TYRA BANKS

**Recent Titles in
Greenwood Biographies**

Jerry Garcia: A Biography
Jacqueline Edmondson

Coretta Scott King: A Biography
Laura T. McCarty

Kanye West: A Biography
Bob Schaller

Peyton Manning: A Biography
Lew Freedman

Miley Cyrus: A Biography
Kimberly Dillon Summers

Ted Turner: A Biography
Michael O'Connor

W. E. B. Du Bois: A Biography
Gerald Horne

George Clooney: A Biography
Joni Hirsch Blackman

Will Smith: A Biography
Lisa M. Iannucci

Toni Morrison: A Biography
Stephanie S. Li

Halle Berry: A Biography
Melissa Ewey Johnson

Osama bin Laden: A Biography
Thomas R. Mockaitis

TYRA BANKS

A Biography

Carole Jacobs

DISCARDED

GREENWOOD BIOGRAPHIES

 GREENWOOD

AN IMPRINT OF ABC-CLIO, LLC
Santa Barbara, California • Denver, Colorado • Oxford, England

Library of Congress Cataloging-in-Publication Data

Jacobs, Carole.
  Tyra Banks : a biography / Carole Jacobs.
    p. cm. — (Greenwood biographies)
  Includes bibliographical references and index.
  ISBN 978–0–313–38274–1 (hard copy : alk. paper) — ISBN 978–0–313–38275–8
  (ebook)
1. Banks, Tyra. 2. African American models—Biography. 3. Models (Person)—
United States—Biography. 4. African American actresses—Biography. 5. African
Americans in television broadcasting—Biography. I. Title.
HD6073.M772U554   2010
746.9′092—dc22   2009050709
[B]

ISBN: 978–0–313–38274–1
EISBN: 978–0–313–38275–8

14 13 12 11 10   1 2 3 4 5

This book is also available on the World Wide Web as an eBook.
Visit www.abc-clio.com for details.

Greenwood
An Imprint of ABC-CLIO, LLC

ABC-CLIO, LLC
130 Cremona Drive, P.O. Box 1911
Santa Barbara, California 93116-1911

This book is printed on acid-free paper ∞

Manufactured in the United States of America

To Tom

CONTENTS

Series Foreword   ix

Preface   xi

Introduction   xvii

Timeline: Events in the Life of Tyra Banks   xxi

Chapter 1   A Star Is Born   1

Chapter 2   The Accidental Supermodel   21

Chapter 3   Lights! Camera! Action!   35

Chapter 4   Supermodel Turned Teen Role Model   49

Chapter 5   From Runway to Reality TV   63

Chapter 6   Tyra's Media Tirades   79

Chapter 7   Tyra Becomes a Media Mogul   93

Chapter 8   False Notes, Dead Ends, and Bad Hair Days   107

Chapter 9   Tyra Enters the Political Arena   123

Chapter 10 Diva or Dreamgirl? The Controversy Continues   135

viii   CONTENTS

Appendix A: Productions and Appearances   151

Appendix B: Awards   165

Selected Bibliography   169

Index   173

Photo essay follows page 78

SERIES FOREWORD

In response to high school and public library needs, Greenwood developed this distinguished series of full-length biographies specifically for student use. Prepared by field experts and professionals, these engaging biographies are tailored for high school students who need challenging yet accessible biographies. Ideal for secondary school assignments, the length, format, and subject areas are designed to meet educators' requirements and students' interests.

Greenwood offers an extensive selection of biographies spanning all curriculum-related subject areas including social studies, the sciences, literature and the arts, history and politics, as well as popular culture, covering public figures and famous personalities from all time periods and backgrounds, both historic and contemporary, who have made an impact on American and/or world culture. Greenwood biographies were chosen based on comprehensive feedback from librarians and educators. Consideration was given to both curriculum relevance and inherent interest. The result is an intriguing mix of the well known and the unexpected, the saints and sinners from long-ago history and contemporary pop culture. Readers will find a wide array of subject choices from fascinating crime figures like Al Capone to inspiring pioneers like Margaret Mead, from the greatest minds of our time like Stephen Hawking to the most amazing success stories of our day like J. K. Rowling.

While the emphasis is on fact, not glorification, the books are meant to be fun to read. Each volume provides in-depth information about the subject's life from birth through childhood, the teen years, and adulthood. A thorough account relates family background and education, traces personal and professional influences, and explores struggles, accomplishments, and contributions. A timeline highlights the most significant life events against a historical perspective. Bibliographies supplement the reference value of each volume.

PREFACE

Tyra Banks is an American media personality, actress, occasional singer, former model, television host and producer, movie producer, and businesswoman who first gained fame as a model in Paris, Milan, London, Tokyo, and New York. At age 19, she broke through long-established racial barriers by becoming the first black model to grace the covers of GQ, the *Sports Illustrated* Swimsuit Issue, and the Victoria's Secret catalogue. Following her runway career, Tyra became a role model for young women by establishing scholarship funds for young, disadvantaged girls, developing summer camps to foster independence and self-esteem in them, and by authoring a self-help book, *Tyra's Beauty Inside & Out*, which became one of School Library Journal's Best Books of 1998. As the creator and host of the UPN/The CW reality television show *America's Next Top Model* and her own talk show, *The Tyra Banks Show*, Tyra became a household name and empire, using her shows as a platform to expose the underside of the modeling and fashion industries and promote confidence in women.

Tyra Lynne Banks was born December 4, 1973, in Inglewood, California, the daughter of Carolyn (née London), a fashion manager and medical photographer, and Donald Banks, a computer consultant. Although Tyra's parents divorced when Tyra was six and both remarried, the relationship among all three remained friendly, with both of Tyra's parents playing a key role in her early success as a supermodel, actress, author, and television host. Tyra graduated from the International School, a private elementary school in Los Angeles, and Immaculate Heart High School, a private girls high school in the Los Feliz neighborhood of Los Angeles. During her adolescent years, Tyra shot to 5´9´´ and lost 20 pounds, bringing her weight to under 100 and leaving her towering over teachers and classmates alike and suffering relentless teasing from her peers, who called her "Lightbulb Head" and "Olive Oyl." During high school, Tyra gained poise and pounds and was encouraged by fellow classmate Khefri Riley, a young model herself, to become a model. After being rejected by four modeling agencies and being told she would never be a cover girl because the camera didn't like her face, Tyra was finally accepted by L.A. Models. While a senior in high school, she switched to Elite Model Agency in Los Angeles and appeared in a fashion shoot for *Seventeen* magazine. Although she planned to attend Loyola Marymount University in the fall, two weeks before classes started she was approached by a French modeling agency to model at the haute couture shows in Paris. When Loyola Marymount offered her a year deferment, Tyra accepted the invitation and quickly broke all records by booking an unprecedented 25 fashion shows in one week during her first season, working with designers Chanel, Christian Dior, and Yves St. Laurent. Within two weeks of arriving in Paris, Tyra also scored her first magazine cover with the French magazine, *20 Ans* (Twenty Years Old).

When Tyra returned home to Los Angeles a year later, modeling offers began pouring in. Her beauty and fame made her a familiar presence in New York, Paris, Milan, and London as she jetted across the world to appear on covers ranging from *Cosmopolitan*, *Vogue*, and *Elle* to *Esquire* and *Harper's Bazaar*. In addition, she signed a lucrative contract with CoverGirl that catapulted her onto the world stage of national television and high-profile fashion magazines. Anxious to expand her image beyond the fashion and modeling industries, Tyra got her big break in 1994 when she landed a recurring role in the popular sitcom, *The Fresh Prince of Bel-Air*, playing opposite actor Will Smith. The role led to Tyra's professional and personal hookup with director John Singleton who cast her in his Hollywood movie, *Higher Learning*.

From the very beginning, Tyra's major goal was to use her fame and fortune as a springboard for helping those less fortunate. After returning home from Paris, she established both the Tyra Banks Scholarship for African American girls at Immaculate Heart High School and Ty Girl Corporation, later named Bankable, Inc. In 1997, Tyra was honored by the Starlight Children's Foundation for her efforts to help underprivileged children. Two years later, she founded TZone, a leadership camp for disadvantaged teenage girls from Los Angeles that she later expanded into an international nonprofit foundation.

In 1999, Oprah Winfrey invited Tyra to join her talk show for two years as a monthly youth correspondent, an experience that whetted Tyra's appetite for TV talk shows. Encouraged by her top ratings on Oprah, in 2003, Tyra launched a new career as a TV reality talk show host with her creation of *America's Next Top Model*, a reality show that combined the best of *American Idol* and *The Real World* into one show about the cutthroat world of modeling. Despite scant initial promotion, the UPN show became an overnight sensation and turned Tyra into an international household name. In 2005, following the advice of mentors Jay Leno and Oprah, Tyra launched her own talk show. *The Tyra Banks Show* quickly became the top-rated show in its time slot among women between the ages of 18 and 35 and established Tyra as the Oprah of her generation.

In 2005, exhausted from a schedule that included modeling as well as producing and hosting two reality shows, Tyra decided to retire from modeling so she could focus on her television career. With her talk show in 190 markets and Tyra owning a hefty stake in it, Tyra was earning upward of $18 million and ranked number 78 on *Forbes's* "Celebrity 100 list." Tyra soon proved she had no plans of becoming just another Oprah. A fearless host, she tackled topics that had never seen the light of day on talk shows, using her platform to expose everything from rampant drug abuse in the modeling industry to society's cruelty toward obese women, which Tyra exposed by donning a 200-pound "fat suit" and walking around Los Angeles. Tyra also used her talk show to debunk myths about herself, inviting a plastic surgeon on her show to give her a very public examination that proved she had never been surgically enhanced. When the Australian paparazzi took unflattering photos of Tyra in a bathing suit that revealed her

30-pound post-runway weight gain and taunted her as "America's Next Top Waddle" and "Tyra Pork Chops," instead of running for cover, Tyra used it as a vehicle to promote self-esteem in women. Climbing into the same bathing suit to appear on her talk show, she told the media to "Kiss my fat ass!" and created the "So What!" campaign to encourage women to accept themselves as they are instead of striving for unrealistic notions of perfection.

In 2007, Tyra signed a long-term production deal with Warner Brothers to develop scripted shows, reality fare, movies, and straight-to-DVD projects. The deal yielded two reality TV shows, both short-lived. *Stylista*, an eight-episode show billed as *The Devil Wears Prada* reinvented as a reality series, starred *Elle* fashion news director Anne Slowey, a real-life meanie charged with eliminating a contestant each week from the show. When *Stylista* wrapped at the end of December 2008 with low ratings, Tyra produced another reality TV show called *True Beauty*, which debuted in January 2009. A beauty competition with a twist, the seven-episode show hosted by former Miss Teen USA Vanessa Minnillo followed contestants who thought they were vying to be named the most physically beautiful person, but were actually, unbeknownst to them, also being judged on their inner beauty, behaviors and kindness, among other criteria. After suffering low ratings and scathing reviews, *True Beauty* followed *Stylista* into obscurity.

Undaunted by the failures of those shows, Tyra entered new talk show turf in 2008 when she became one of the few television programs to conduct one-hour interviews with leading presidential candidates, including Senator Barack Obama, Senator Hillary Clinton, Governor Mike Huckabee, and Senator John Edwards. Millions tuned in to hear Tyra chat up Hillary about Bill's affair, offer to read Obama's palm, and badger Mike Huckabee about his stance on gay marriage and abortion. But Tyra's talk show ratings hit the ionosphere when she invited Levi Johnson, Bristol Palin's ex-boyfriend and father of her illegitimate son, to come on her program and spill the beans about life with Sarah Palin.

The recipient of hundreds of awards, including *People* magazine's "100 Most Beautiful People," *Glamour* magazine's "Woman of the Year," and *Forbes*'s "20 Top-Earning Women," in 2008 Tyra achieved the pinnacle of talk show host success by earning an Emmy for her day-time talk show—the first one ever awarded in the category of information. With two hit TV shows and past accomplishments ranging from supermodel and actor to author, producer, entrepreneur, and philanthropist, Tyra says she's just warming up. She's already branched out with her own fashion, cosmetic, and fragrance lines and hopes to build an Oprah-like empire within the next ten years.

INTRODUCTION

Unlike other celebrities who hide behind a veil of secrecy or a wall of handlers, what you see is pretty much what you get with Tyra Banks, whether it's her much publicized "fat ass" or the pesky cellulite that, during an interview on her talk show with the presidential candidate, she claimed to share with Hillary Clinton. Love her or hate her, Tyra has earned a reputation of telling it like it is—or at least as she sees it, regardless of the media firestorm or mountains of hate mail her opinions generate.

But what distinguishes Tyra most from other supermodels and celebrities is her willingness and, at times, even her insistence, to expose her personal flaws, mistakes, and insecurities and to use them to connect with girls and women who struggle with self-esteem issues.

A tireless opponent of "the big lie" foisted on a generation of unwitting women by the modeling and fashion industries, Tyra uses her talk show as a platform to publicly debunk the myth of perfect beauty, often using herself as an example of what makeup artists can create or hide by appearing on her show without a trace of it on. By letting millions of women in on the lie, Tyra has empowered them to accept themselves as they are instead of striving for unrealistic notions of perfection. Tyra took things one step further on *The Tyra Banks Show*, introducing "The Sisterhood Initiative" as a way to bring women closer together and minimize the competition and rivalry that is often a by-product of the beauty myth. "Too often I feel like we hate each other—we find the negative, and we allow guys to polarize us. I'm sick of it!" she recently told *Redbook*.[1]

Tyra is also a rarity in an industry rife with greed and conspicuous spending. From the beginning of her modeling career at age 19, Tyra began donating her time and money to help underprivileged children and teens, working one-on-one rather than merely lending her name to the cause. Recalling her awkward and geeky adolescent and teenage years, she also created a summer camp program for disadvantaged teenage girls designed to enhance their self-esteem. The camps were later transitioned into a grant-making organization for building a sisterhood movement—referring to their interest in building an organization that promotes and defends the rights of all women. Tyra also wrote a self-help book for teenage girls to empower them to accomplish whatever they wanted in life, including, "most of all, learning to love yourself."[2]

Early on in her career, Tyra set herself apart from the modeling and Hollywood brat pack by becoming an outspoken critic of smoking, drinking, and drug use, turning down millions of dollars of offers to promote cigarettes and alcohol while exposing herself to ridicule for her goody two-shoed teetotaler ways.

In fact, the more famous Tyra became, the more she became a target for the media's slings and arrows. When her reality TV show, *America's Next Top Model*, became an overnight hit, critics hit below the belt, claiming Tyra's success had not only gone to her head but also to her butt. In a cry heard, if not 'round the world then, at least by every overweight woman on the planet, Tyra told the paparazzi to "kiss my fat ass!" when they snapped photos revealing her 30-pound post-runway gain, splashed them across tabloids, and crowned her "America's Next Top Waddle."[3]

Meanwhile, on reality TV, there were growing mumblings *America's Next Top Model*, which purports to help young women achieve their wildest supermodel dreams, was actually a cruel hoax that gave contestants false hopes and promises while substantially padding Tyra's pocketbook. When Tyra branched out with her own Oprah-like talk show, claiming she hoped to become the voice of her generation, the press went for the jugular, claiming Tyra was everything from phony and inept to a hypocrite who preaches dignity and can't-touch-this-fierceness while exploiting sexual material to increase her ratings.[4]

Throughout it all, Tyra has maintained her trademark chutzpa, taking the bullets publicly rather than ducking for cover. In the "Top Waddle" incident, instead of racing to a plastic surgeon for lipo, she turned herself into an example and created the "So What!" campaign. While Tyra admitted the "top waddle" media storm was humiliating and embarrassing, it also served to solidify her reputation of telling it like it is—something she plans to keep doing, regardless of the medium.

"It's not like I want to be a perfect role model," Tyra told *Redbook*. "I know I'll make mistakes. It'll be all over the headlines and I'll have to deal with that. But now people are really looking at the real me, and it feels so good."[5]

NOTES

1. Quoted by Juan Morales, "Tyra Banks," *Redbook*, April 2006: 138.

2. Tyra Banks, *Tyra's Beauty Inside & Out* (New York: Harper Collins, 1998), 17–18.

3. Lacey Rose, "Prime-Time TV's 20 Top-Earning Women," *Forbes*, September 2008, www.forbes.com/2008/08/28/television-actresses-hollywood-biz-media-cx_lr_0902tvstars.html (accessed June 30, 2008).

4. Ned Martel. "For the Most Part, Far from the Modeling Crowd," *New York Times*, November 2, 2005, www.nytimes.com/2005/11/02/arts/television/02mart.html?_r=1 (accessed July 24, 2009).

5. Quoted by Morales, "Tyra Banks," 139.

TIMELINE: EVENTS IN THE LIFE OF TYRA BANKS

December 4, 1973 Tyra Lynn Banks is born in Inglewood, California, the daughter of Carolyn (née London), a fashion manager and medical photographer, and Donald Banks, a computer consultant.

September 1979 Tyra enters International Children's School, a private elementary school in Los Angeles.

March 1980 Tyra's parents divorce when Tyra is six, although the relationship with her parents and especially her brother Devin Banks stays friendly.

1983 Tyra experiences a rash of skin problems, including warts that developed on both her hands. Tyra tried to hide her hands by wearing gloves, but her classmates teased her relentlessly and called her "Froggy, Froggy!"

Tyra's beloved grandmother, Florine London, dies at age 50 after a painful bout with lung cancer. Tyra watched her painful death and vowed she would never smoke. As a model, she refused any and all offers to promote smoking or cigarette ads.

Tyra feels betrayed when her mother remarries Clifford Johnson, Jr., a high school graphics art teacher.

May 1984 Tyra graduates from the International Children's School.

September 1985 Tyra enrolls at John Burroughs High School, a public school in Los Angeles, but found the school's large campus and large class sizes intimidating.

1985 At age 12, Tyra has a growth spurt, shooting up to 5´ 9´´ and losing 20 pounds in three months time to weigh 98 pounds. Towering over the other students and even her teachers, she becomes the butt of jokes and is teased relentlessly by her classmates, who call her "Olive Oyl" and "Lighthead Bulb." Tyra, once outgoing and extroverted, withdraws and becomes shy, awkward, and introverted. In an attempt to gain weight, she gorges on junk foods and fried foods and drinks a chocolate-and-peanut butter milkshake before bedtime every night, but the scale won't budge beyond "98."

September 1987 Tyra enrolls at Immaculate Heart High School, a private girl's high school in the Los Feliz neighborhood of Los Angeles. Although she initially feels out of place, she soon makes new friends and finds the absence of boys a bonus because she doesn't have to worry about dressing up to impress them.

Tyra befriends fellow classmate Khefri Riley, who invites her to join her in frequenting thrift shops and encourages Tyra to become a model.

April 1989 After being rejected by four modeling agencies —one said they already had a black model while another one said the camera didn't like her face—Tyra is overjoyed when she is invited to join L.A. Models in Los Angeles, her first modeling agency.

February 1990 Tyra, now a high school senior, is selected by *Seventeen* magazine through L.A. Models to be photographed for an upcoming issue. The editor of the magazine was so impressed with Tyra's portfolio that she hired her on the spot and sent a photo crew to meet her and photograph her for the March 1991 issue.

September 1990 An unknown Tyra Banks appears on the cover of *Marie Claire* (France).

March 1991 Tyra signs with Elite Model Agency in Los Angeles.

Tyra appears in a fashion shoot in *Seventeen* magazine.

May 1991 Tyra graduates from Immaculate Heart High School. Having been accepted at five different colleges, including UCLA and USC in Los Angeles, she decides to go to Loyola Marymont in Los Angeles, where she plans to major in film. Tyra appears in Michael Jackson's "Black or White" music video in the sequence of celebrity cameos.

August 1991 Two weeks before she was to enter Loyola Marymount, a French modeling agency offered to sponsor her for a year to model at the haute couture shows in Paris, Tyra decided to put her college career on hold. Loyola Marymount gives her a year deferment. Her mother is admittedly nervous about Tyra's decision to postpone college but gives her daughter her full support and coaches her on walking down the runway. To practice, Tyra parades back and forth in the living room in her mother's high heels and nightgowns.

September 1991	Tyra flies from Los Angeles to Paris and begins working as a model.
Fall 1991	Tyra breaks all records by booking for an unprecedented 25 fashion shows in one week during her first season, working with designers Chanel, Christian Dior, and Yves St. Laurent. Within two weeks of arriving in Paris, she gets her first magazine cover with the French magazine, *20 Ans* (Twenty Years Old).
Winter 1991	Desperately homesick, shunned by fellow models for her refusal to drink, smoke, do drugs, and hang out, and rebuked by a jealous and threatened Naomi Campbell, who had Tyra barred from working a Chanel show, Tyra begs her mother to join her in Paris. To overcome her longing for home, she frequented fast-food joints in Paris and lived on care packages her mother sent, which contained Tyra's favorite American snacks, such as peanut brittle and caramel.
	Tyra's mother, urged by the modeling agency to come to Paris because of her daughter's overnight success, reluctantly quits her job and moves to Paris to manage her daughter's fledging modeling career.
August 1992	Tyra graces the cover of *Harper's Bazaar*. (Germany).
October 1992	Tyra and her mother Carolyn leave Paris and return to Los Angeles.
	Anxious to use her newfound fame to help those less fortunate, Tyra becomes the spokesperson for the Center for Children + Families in New York City and does a series of lectures on race, beauty, and body image in the modeling industry.
	Using $10,000 she had earned in Paris, Tyra establishes the Tyra Banks Scholarship Fund

for girls at Immaculate Heart High and founds Ty Girl Corporation.

October 1992 Tyra appears on the cover of *Elle* magazine (Spain).

November 1992 Tyra appears in the British television movie, *Inferno*, starring several supermodels.

April 1993 After seeing her on the cover of a magazine, John Singleton, director of *Boyz 'n the Hood*, gets friends to introduce him to Tyra. It is love at first sight.

May 1993 Tyra becomes the third black female model with a lucrative modeling contract with CoverGirl cosmetics.

June 1993 Tyra graces the cover of *Essence*.

December 1993 Following a wrenching personal experience involving a man named Theo who was dying of AIDS, Tyra arranged to meet him and said he "opened my eyes, not only to AIDS but to our shared humanity." As a result of that encounter, Tyra became a spokeswoman for the Pediatric AIDS Foundation.

January 1994 Tyra is featured on the cover of *Elle* magazine (Spain).

May 1994 Named one of the "50 Most Beautiful People in the World" by *People* magazine.

September 1994 Auditioning in her trademark jeans, T-shirt, and athletic shoes, Tyra lands a breakout role playing Jackie Ames for seven episodes in the hit TV series, *The French Prince of Bel Air*. At 5′ 11″, she was the perfect height to play opposite actor Will Smith, who is 6′2″. Tyra said being on television made her more accessible to the public than modeling had because people were no longer intimidated by her.

December 1994 Tyra graces the cover of *Elle* magazine for the third time.

January 1995	Tyra plays "Deja," a student and track runner at a university, in *Higher Learning*. Because the movie was directed by Tyra's boyfriend at the time, John Singleton, some people in the media claimed she had gotten the role because of her relationship with him. But Singleton set the record straight, insisting he had hired Tyra for her acting talent.
March 1995	Tyra breaks up with John Singleton.
July 1995	Tyra graces the cover of *Max* magazine (United Kingdom edition).
January 1996	Tyra shares the cover of the *Sports Illustrated* Swimsuit Issue with model Valeria Mazza.
February 1996	Tyra becomes the first woman and the first black model to grace the cover of *GQ*.
March 1996	Tyra briefly dates pop singer Seal, who later marries supermodel and Tyra's friend Heidi Klum. Seal's breakup with Tyra provided some of the emotional fire for his 1998 album, *Human Being*, which included a song begging for forgiveness called "When a Man Is Wrong."
	Tyra begins appearing in television commercials, including Nike's 'L'il Penny, McDonald's "Gone Fishin'" and milk mustache print ads for the National Milk Processor Promotion Board.
April 1996	*People* magazine names Tyra one of the "100 Most Beautiful People in the World."
May 1996	Tyra appears on the cover of *Anna* magazine (Italy).
November 1996	Tyra graces the cover of *TV-Spielfilm* magazine (Germany).
December 1996	Tyra is featured on the cover of *GQ* (Spain).
	Tyra appears on the cover of *Black Men*.
January 1997	Tyra becomes a spokesperson for the Center for Children & Families in Los Angeles.

Awarded "Friendship Award" by Starlight Foundation for her charitable work with underprivileged children.

February 1997 Tyra becomes the first African American model to be featured solo on the *Sports Illustrated* Swimsuit Issue.

Signs exclusive contract with Swatch watches.

March 1997 Tyra graces the cover of *Fitness* magazine.

Tyra renames Ty Girl Corporation as Bankable, Inc.

Tyra establishes Kidshare event in Los Angeles for needy children.

April 1997 Has a small role in the movie, *A Woman Like That.*

May 1997 Tyra wins a Michael Award for Supermodel of the Year, which honors the brightest of the fashion industry and benefits the National Children's Leukemia Foundation.

Receives Friendship Award from the Starlight Children's Foundation in Los Angeles for her charitable work with underprivileged children.

Graces the cover of *Cosmopolitan* (Germany).

Appears on the cover of *Details* magazine.

July 1997 Appears on the cover of *Cosmopolitan* magazine (Germany).

August 1997 Appears on the cover of *Maxim* magazine.

September 1997 Appears in three episodes of *New York Undercover.*

Appears on the cover of *Man* magazine (Spain).

October 1997 Tyra signs an exclusive contract with Victoria's Secret and becomes the first black model to grace their catalogue cover.

November 1997 Appears on the cover of *Photo* magazine (France).

December 1997 Featured on the cover of *Shape* magazine.

February 1998 Stars as herself in the movie, *Elmopalooza!*

March 1998   Receiving thousands of fan letters each year, Tyra decides to answer many of her fans' beauty and fashion questions by writing a book. *Tyra's Beauty Inside & Out* combines beauty and fashion tips with essays written by Tyra on topics ranging from love and sex to the importance of volunteering. The book is named one of School Library Journal's Best Books of 1998.

Tyra appears on the *Howard Stern* show.

April 1998   Appears on the cover of *Seventeen* magazine.

July 1998   Appears on the cover of *Cosmopolitan* magazine (Spain).

Appears on cover of *Photo* magazine (France).

November 1998   Tyra tries her hand at producing for the Disney TV movie, *Honey Thunder Dunk*. She coproduces it and also has a starring role in the movie.

Develops the first official Tyra Banks Web site, www.tyratyratyra.com.

December 1998   Serves as maid of honor for best friend, Kimora Lee, at her wedding to Russell Simmons.

January 1999   Appears on the cover of *GQ* magazine.

February 1999   Joins *Oprah* show for a two-year stint as monthly "youth correspondent."

April 1999   Graces the cover of *P.O.V.* magazine.

July 1999   Appears on the cover of *Just for Black Men* magazine.

March 1999   Hosts the 13th Annual Soul Train Music Awards.

September 1999   Portrays "Holly Garnett" in the romantic comedy, *Love Stinks*, about a struggling sitcom writer who finally gets to date his dream girl, but she turns out to be a nightmare. Holly is the best friend of the psychotic dream girl.

October 1999   Has a small role in the TV movie, *The Apartment Complex*.

January 2000   Founds TZone, a summer camp program in the
                San Bernardino Mountains above Los Angeles
                for disadvantaged teenage girls in Los Angeles.
                Has a recurring role as "Natasha Claybourne" on
                Fox TV's *New York Undercover*.
                Has two guest appearances on *Mad TV* as
                "Katisha."
                Appears in three episodes of *Felicity* playing
                "Jane Scott."
                Joins up with supermodels such as Carol Alt and
                Marla Maples in a charity event to help fight
                infant AIDS in Atlanta during Super Bowl
                week. The models help out with spa duties
                which cost patrons $300 per session.
                Teams up with basketball star Kobe Bryant in a
                musical duet for NBC for the single "K-O-B-E,"
                which was featured on his debut album.

February 2000   Appears in George Michael's video, *Too Funky*.
                Comes in second place to Cindy Crawford in the
                "1999 Sally Beauty Supply's Best Tressed Celeb-
                rity Survey," which polled 1,000 American's
                over 18.
                Appears on the cover of *People*.

March 2000   Portrays "Eve" in Walt Disney's TV movie *Life-
                Size*, with up-and-coming Lindsay Lohan.
                Does the Oscar warm-up show and interviews
                Angelina Jolie and Salma Hayek.

April 2000   Plays "Kyra Kessler" in the movie, *Love and
                Basketball*, a romantic drama about two aspiring
                basketball players and next-door neighbors who
                fight off and on the court while falling in love.

June 2000   Tyra is interviewed in *Vibe* about dating and
                boyfriends.

July 2000   Appears on the cover of *Celebrity Sleuth*.
                Featured on the cover of *Just for Black Men*.

August 2000   Graces the cover of *Maxim*.

Plays "Zoe" in *Coyote Ugly*, a sex comedy about an aspiring songwriter who comes of age while working at a bar filled with wild women.

Takes part in the Magic Johnson Foundation hosted 15th Annual "A Midsummer Night's Magic" fundraising weekend August 4–6 in Los Angeles.

September 2000   Tyra stars, as herself, in the special *Sports Illustrated Swimsuit Collection 1995–1999*.

October 2000   Featured in *Maxim* Magazine's Models 2000's "Five for the Ages," where the magazine highlights the fact that Tyra has appeared on more than 20 magazine covers to date.

November 2000   Develops official Tyra Banks Web site, www.tyratyratyra.com.

Wins $125,000 in the *Celebrity Who Wants to Be A Millionaire* on ABC. Tyra plays for her own charity, TZone. Tyra's mother was on hand and she used her brother for the phone-a-friend portion of the game.

December 2000   Tyra became the first African American model to grace the covers of both *GQ*, for which she was also named "Woman of the Year—2000," and the *Sports Illustrated* Swimsuit Issues in 1996 and 1997.

Tyra ranks #15 in *Playboy*'s list of The Sex Stars 2000.

Appears in the movie, *O Brother, Where Art Thou?*

February 2001   Tyra arranges for her mother to get a makeover on the Oprah show.

An abstracts.net poll reports that 81 percent of visitors to the site thought Tyra was the world's most beautiful African American woman.

April 2001   Appears as "Miss April" on *Maxim* magazine's 2001 15-month calendar.

May 2001	Ranks number 33 in FHM's 100 Sexiest Women in the World 2001 edition, voted on by readers. Tyra was at number 5 the previous year.
	Joins the cast of Jamie Foxx's variety show pilot on The WB called *These Nuts*.
June 2001	Featured in a rare French magazine, *Miss Ebene*, that is up for bids on Ebay.
August 2001	Heads up to TZone camp in the San Bernardino mountains above LA, having funded the camp through her "win" on *Celebrity Millionaire*. Tyra devotes her summer to the camp, interacting one-on-one with girls and offering them help and advice. Many campers assumed they'd either never see Tyra or that she'd only pop in for a quick visit.
November 2001	Helps close the New York Stock Exchange Thursday, November 15, with Sharen Turney, president and CEO of Victoria's Secret Direct, by ringing the closing bell.
December 2001	Sells her Los Angeles-area penthouse condo, getting close to the $1.2 million she asked for her two-bedroom pad.
February 2002	Tyra is spotted consistently at Sacramento Kings basketball games and is later confirmed to be dating their forward Chris Webber. Though their representatives deny, rumors swirl that the two are engaged.
March 2002	Has a small role in the Hollywood comedy, *Larceny*.
May 2002	Appears on the cover of *Ocean Drive*.
June 2002	Graces the cover of *Arena* (UK).
July 2002	Appears on cover of *TV direct* (Germany).
	Plays "Nora Winston" in the movie *Halloween: Resurrection*, the eighth in a series of horror flicks starring actors like Jamie Lee Curtis and Sean Patrick Thomas.

September 2002	Plays a supermodel in the movie *Fashiontrance*. Appears on the cover of *Ebony*.
November 2002	Walks the runway at the Victoria Secret Fashion Show at the Lexington Avenue Armory in New York City.
	Graces the cover of *TV Guide*.
	Plays the voice of the "Victoria Secret Gown" in Adam Sandler's *Eight Crazy Nights*, an animated musical comedy about a slacker in trouble with the law who must referee a basketball league for community service.
December 2002	Has a small role in the movie *Cleavage*.
February 2003	Appears as a guest on *Dees Hotline* to talk about TZone, her self-esteem building camp for teen girls.
March 2003	Tries to establish herself as a singer by airing her music video, "Shake Ya Body" on the taping of *America's Next Top Model*. Unfortunately, the single went nowhere, despite her efforts and work with Mariah Carey and Janet Jackson to improve her voice. Tyra spent $30,000 of her own money to finance the music video.
May 2003	Launches her reality TV show, *America's Next Top Model*, on the fledging UPN network, serving as hostess, arm judge, and executive producer with Ken Mok. Tyra taps friends and fellow supermodels Janice Dickinson and Kimora Lee Simmons to serve as judges for the program. The crew has just one month to find and shoot contestants for the first season before preproduction begins. Season 1 ends with Adrianne Curry winning the title of *America's Next Top Model*. After leaving the show, Curry becomes publicly critical of Tyra, claiming she is nasty and two-faced.

Appears on *Late Night with Conan O'Brien* to plug her new UPN show and reveals she's now 143 pounds.

Named number 38 on *Maxim* magazine's "Hot 100 for 2003" list. Christina Aguilera topped the list.

Graces the cover of *Stuff* magazine.

June 2003   Appears as a guest on *Jimmy Kimmel Live*.

August 2003   Has a small role in the movie, *Totally Gay!*

Throws the first pitch at Comerica Park in Detroit before the Detroit Tigers vs. Texas Rangers game on Wednesday (August 20) in Detroit, Michigan.

October 2003   Honored at *Health Magazine*'s "Beauty Awards Luncheon" held at the Rainbow Room in New York City.

November 2003   Appears in the televised "2003 Victoria's Secret Fashion Show" with Heidi Klum, Gisele Bündchen, Mary J. Blige, Eve, Sting, Pharrell Williams, Sean 'P. Diddy' Combs, Damon Dash, and Tommy Lee.

Appears as a guest on *The View*.

Appears as a guest on the CBS *Early Show*.

December 2003   Graces the cover of *People*.

February 2004   Appears as a guest on the *Ellen DeGeneres Show*.

March 2004   Performs as Velvelette of The Velvelettes during a taping of *American Dreams*.

UPN announces that Tyra's video for her single, "Shake Ya Body," has gotten 155,000 hits on the UPN Web site since it debuted on *America's Next Top Model*.

Appears on the cover of *TV Guide*.

April 2004   Appears on the cover of *King* magazine and says, "My whole body is insured."

Talks to *Steppin' Out Magazine* about her music career.

May 2004   Graces the cover of *Ebony* magazine.

August 2004	Appears as a guest star at the 2004 Teen Choice Awards along with Jessica Alba, Lindsay Lohan, Paris Hilton, Paula Abdul, and others.
September 2004	Tyra becomes a media mogul, signing a multimillion-dollar deal with Telepictures to host her own daytime talk show, to be executive produced by Benny Medina.
	In Touch magazine reports that Tyra Banks and Chris Webber are close to marrying.
	Tyra breaks up with Chris Webber after almost three years, but the two remain friends.
October 2004	Tyra models the Victoria' Secret's 2004 Heavenly 70 Fantasy Bra by Mouawad, featuring a 70-carat flawless pear-shaped diamond in the center. The one-of-a-kind bra is worth $10 million.
December 2004	Produces the TV Movie, *Marple: The Body in the Library*, based on an Agatha Christie Novel.
January 2005	Appears on the cover of *Vibe*.
June 2005	Named to *Forbes* magazine's "Celebrity 100 Power Ranking."
September 2005	Launches her daytime talk show, *The Tyra Banks Show*. The show premieres in front of a live audience at Chelsea Studios in New York City after having been previously taped at CBS Television in Los Angeles. In a nod to her past career as a model, Tyra has guests make their appearance by walking down a runway.
	Tyra graces the cover of *Self* magazine.
October 2005	Tyra announces on her talk show that she is retiring from modeling and devoting herself full time to her two reality shows. Her mother, Carolyn, surprises Tyra by inviting family and friends on the show to help celebrate.
November 2005	Tyra appears in her last Victoria's Secret fashion show in New York City, donning a red lace bra and underwear made of military medallions.

Fellow supermodels working the show, including Naomi Campbell, Gisele Bündchen, and Heidi Klum, talk Tyra into taking her angel wings home with her as a farewell gift.

Tyra invites fellow supermodel Naomi Campbell on her talk show to publicly bury the hatchet, ending a years-long feud that has festered since Tyra's early modeling days in Paris.

Wearing a full-body "fat suit," Tyra goes undercover as an obese woman and parades around Los Angeles in an attempt to experience what it's like to be an obese woman in our thin-obsessed society.

February 2006 Tyra takes her talk show to Las Vegas, where she transform into a sexy Vegas showgirl and joins the cast of Jubilee for their opening number wearing a G-string, rhinestone bar, and headdress.

Tyra is overjoyed to learn that her talk show will be renewed by UPN for a second season.

March 2006 Tyra goes undercover as "Chanel" for her talk show topic on why men frequent strip clubs.

April 2006 Appears on the cover of *Redbook* magazine.

June 2006 Featured in *Forbes* magazine's cover story, "Tyra Banks on It."

Tyra ranks number 84 on the *Forbes* Celebrity 100 list of top earners, and tops *Fortune*'s list of top women earners in entertainment, earning a reported $23 million.

Tyra graces the cover of *Lucky* magazine.

January 2007 An unflattering photo of Tyra on vacation in Sydney shows the supermodel's increasing curves and sets off a media firestorm. The Australian tabloids call her "America's Next Top Waddle" and "Porkchops."

February 2007 Tyra retaliates against the media circus surrounding her weight gain since her modeling days, mounting a "So What" campaign and telling the media to "Kiss my fat ass!"

April 2007 Stung by the media circus surrounding her weight gain, Tyra goes on *The View* to discuss her "So What" campaign and is cheered by the audience.

May 2007 Appears on the *CW11 Morning Talk Show* in New York City.

Appears again on *The View* and playfully feels up Rosie O'Donnell, asking her if she has implants.

Appears on *Late Night with Conan O'Brien.*

Linked with Knicks coach Isiah Thomas after seen lunching with him in New York.

Appears on *Good Morning America* to discuss unflattering tabloid photos.

Appears on *Good Day New York* to discuss upcoming program schedule.

Appears on the cover of *Time* magazine, who names her one of its "100 Influential People of the Year."

June 2007 Saluted as a trailblazer and receives a BET Honors Award for her work in media alongside Time Warner CEO Richard Parsons and other notables.

Produces *The Clique*, her first DVD-to-movie based on the best-selling young adult's book series.

July 2007 Appears on the cover of *Tros Kompas* (Netherlands).

September 2007 Chosen by *FTC Publications Class-Elite Magazine* as "The Role Model for Models."

Tyra denies rumors she is engaged to her boyfriend, New York investment banker John Utendahl.

Tyra calls in to *KIIS FM* with Ryan Seacrest to discuss her upcoming season of *America's Next Top Model.*

Appears on *Good Day LA* to discuss third season of her talk show.

In her first presidential interview, Tyra talks to Democratic presidential candidate Barack Obama on her talk show, asking him soft questions about his first date with his wife and dropping hints that she wants to spend a night at the White House, which Barack politely ignores. Although media wags criticize Tyra for venturing into unfamiliar turf, Tyra announces that she has invited all the candidates to appear on her show. With the exception of Republican presidential candidates John McCain and Mitt Romney, they all do.

Tyra once again graces the cover of *Ebony* magazine.

Appears in *V* magazine editorial as a rising star.

October 2007   Tyra signs a long-term production deal with Warner Bros. to develop scripted shows, reality fare, movies, and straight-to-DVD projects.

November 2007   *The Tyra Banks Show* airs her infamous "vagina puppet" program and triggers a media frenzy.

December 2007   Appears on *Showbiz Tonight*.
Tyra is a "Tribute presenter" for CNN's *Heroes*.
Tyra reveals her desire to adopt a baby.

January 2008   Tyra interviews Democratic presidential candidate John Edwards. The former senator talked about having to work a bit harder than the other candidates in order to get his message to be heard.

Tyra also interviews Democratic presidential candidate Hillary Clinton on her talk show. Hillary gets frank about what happened when her husband's, then president Bill Clinton, marital infidelity was revealed, and why she decided to stay with him. When she tells Tyra she has cellulite, Tyra admits she also has lots of it.

February 2008	Appears on the cover of *Entertainment Weekly* under the headline, "Tyra Inc. She's Building An Empire. Just Don't Call Her Oprah Jr." *America's Next Top Model* enters its 10th season. Tyra interviews Republican presidential candidate Mike Huckabee on her talk show. After grilling him about gay marriage, she stops being so aggressive for a friendly jam session with him.
March 2008	Appears on cover of the *New York Times Magazine* in a piece titled "Martha, Oprah, Tyra; Is She the Next Big Female Branded Self?" Named by *Hollywood Reporter*'s list of "100 Most Powerful Women in Entertainment." Presented the "Excellence in Media Award by GLADD at its 20th Annual GLAAD Media Awards in New York City.
April 2008	Appears on *The View*. Purchases a bamboo-floored apartment in Manhattan's trendy, energy-efficient Riverhouse, where Leonardo DiCaprio also has an apartment.
June 2008	Wins her first Daytime Emmy Award for "Outstanding Talk Show/Informative." Appears in award-winning documentary, *All of Us*, by Emily Abt.
August 2008	Plays herself in Ben Stiller's hit comedy, *Tropic Thunder*.
September 2008	Portrays Michelle Obama in a *Harpers Bazaar* photo spread. Honored by *Cosmopolitan* magazine as one of its "2008 Fun Fearless Phenom" Award winners. Named to *Forbes*'s magazine list of Primetime TV's 20 Top-Earning Women, topping the list with a reported $23 million in earnings.
October 2008	Tyra's new reality TV show, *Stylista*, debuts in what the media calls a merging of *The Devil Wears Prada* with reality TV. The show is hosted

by Anne Slowey, the real-life fashion editor of *Elle* magazine, and shot in a fake magazine office because the producers didn't think Elle's digs were glam enough.

November 2008   Named one of *Glamour* magazine's "2008 Glamour Women of the Year" along with Nicole Kidman and Hillary Clinton.

Officially backs Barack Obama as president.

Airs controversial talk show episode in which she offers to pay for a sex change operation for transgender Isis King, a former contestant on *America's Next Top Model*.

December 2008   Named by *Entertainment Weekly* as one of "25 Smartest in Television."

Appears on the cover of *Ebony* magazine.

January 2009   Tyra's new reality TV show, *True Beauty*, debuts. The eight-episode show is hosted by former Miss Teen USA Vanessa Minnillo and gets lukewarm ratings and reviews. Minnillo confesses to *TV Guide* that the contestants were rude and ill-mannered, even when they caught on that the underlying but unstated premise of the show was that inner beauty was far more important than outer beauty.

February 2009   Appears on the cover of *Elle Girl* magazine.

March 2009   Brady Green, 39, of Dublin, Georgia, is arrested on March 18 for stalking Tyra. When Green is arrested at a McDonald's restaurant near Tyra's Manhattan studio, he tells officers they "had a thing together," police said. Green's lawyer Sydney O'Hagen defended his client as an "overzealous fan."

April 2009   Interviews Levi Johnson on her talk show. Johnson fathered the illegitimate son of Bristol Palin, daughter of former Alaska governor and Republican vice presidential candidate Sarah Palin. Johnson shocks the audience by telling

Tyra that the Alaskan governor not only knew they were shacking up at her house, but "probably knew me and Bristol were having sex."

Tyra's stalker, Brady Green, is convicted of stalking, harassment, criminal trespass and attempted aggravated harassment against Tyra. Green was convicted of stalking Tyra from coast to coast—calling her offices, showing up at her TV studios, and sending her flowers. Police said he threatened to cut a staffer's throat for not telling him where Banks was.

May 2009	Fires Paulina Porizkova from her hosting gig on *America's Next Top Model* citing budgetary problems. The firing unleashes a storm of controversy from former judge Janice Dickinson.
June 2009	Nominated for a Daytime Emmy for Outstanding Talk Show/Informative for *The Tyra Banks Show*.

Brady Green, Tyra's stalker and least favorite fan, is sentenced to a year of probation and ordered to complete a treatment program designed specifically for stalkers. Green is also ordered to stay away from Tyra for the next two years under an order of protection or face up to 90 days in jail if he disobeys any of the court's orders.

July 2008	Featured in the all-black issue of *Italian Vogue*.
August 2009	Appears as herself in *Hannah Montana: The Movie*.
September 2009	Tyra's talk show is taken out of syndication and moves to The CW for its fifth season, joining *America's Next Top Model* on the same network.

Chapter 1

A STAR IS BORN

Tyra Lynn Banks was born at 7:14 p.m. on December 4, 1973, in Inglewood, California, a close-knit, middle-class, predominantly black neighborhood located just south of downtown Los Angeles and about five miles from the Pacific Ocean. She was the second child and first daughter of Carolyn and Don Banks, a medical photographer at the Jet Propulsion Lab in La Canada, and computer consultant, respectively.[1]

At the hospital where Tyra was born, her grandmother overheard a long Asian name from a Filipino woman, but only liked part of the name—and promptly named the baby girl, "Tyra." Tyra went home with her parents to a small, cozy home in Inglewood, where her six-year-old brother, Devin, had been excitedly waiting to meet her.[2] If Tyra's unusual first name was a stumbling block for Tyra in grade school and high school, where teachers and classmates had trouble spelling her name, it would one day become a valuable asset to Tyra in branding herself as one of America's top models and reality TV show hosts. Like Oprah, Cher, and Martha, Tyra would become part of that elite club of celebrities who are so famous they don't need last names to be recognized.

When Tyra was born, her hometown of Inglewood was celebrating its 100th anniversary. Founded in 1873 and incorporated in 1908, Inglewood began as a quiet poultry farming town. As the Los Angeles metropolitan area expanded, Inglewood's poultry farms were plowed under to create beautiful residential suburbs for workers commuting into the city. Due to its centralized location between downtown Los Angeles and the coast, Inglewood was considered a highly desirable place for young families to live and raise children. With the construction of the Greater Western Forum sports arena in the mid-1960s, Inglewood became a well-known sports Mecca, and home to several professional sports teams, including the Los Angeles Lakers basketball team and the Los Angeles Kings hockey team. Inglewood's Hollywood Park racetrack also lured hoards of horseracing fans. It was in this exciting and vibrant community that young Tyra grew up.[3]

THE DECADE OF HUMAN RIGHTS

Tyra was born in a decade that celebrated women's rights, including the rights of black women and women of race. When she was five years old, Coretta Scott King, the courageous feminist who had inherited the leadership position of the civil rights movement from her husband as leader of the black movement, called for an end to all discrimination and helped encourage the Woman's Liberation movement and other movements as well. At the National Women's Conference in 1977 a minority women's resolution, promoted by King and others, was passed to ensure racial equality in the movement's goals, after which, in one of the most emotional moments of the conference, women of all races joined hands and sang, "We Shall Overcome."

During the 1970s as Tyra was growing up, the role of women in society was profoundly altered with growing feminism across the world and with the presence and rise of a significant number of women as heads of state outside of monarchies and heads of government in a number of countries across the world, many of whom were the first women to hold such positions. In 1979, when Tyra was six, Margaret Thatcher became the United Kingdom's first woman prime minister in 1979. In 1980, when Tyra was seven, Indira Gandhi was reelected as prime minister of India. Both Indira Gandhi and Margaret Thatcher would remain important political figures in the 80s as Tyra became a young adult and woman.

During the 1970s, the women's movement was also reflected on TV in new shows about single women in "traditionally male" careers, such as *The Mary Tyler Moore Show*. By the mid- to late-1970s, programs like *Charlie's Angels* and *Three's Company* had introduced open sexuality and bawdy humor into TV.[4]

The 1970s was also an exciting time for blacks in the music and entertainment industry, with the further rise of such popular, influential rhythm and blues (R&B) artists as multi-instrumentalist Stevie Wonder and the popular quintet The Jackson 5. The mid-1970s also saw the rise of disco music, which dominated during the last half of the decade with black musicians such as Donna Summer. Towards the end of the decade, Jamaican reggae music, already popular in the Caribbean and Africa since the early 1970s, became a big hit in the United States and in Europe, mostly because of reggae superstar and legend Bob Marley.[5]

By the time Tyra had become a supermodel, it was clear she had absorbed the lessons of her childhood heroines. Like them, Tyra succeeded in breaking down racial barriers not only for herself, but also for all women of color.

DADDY'S LITTLE GIRL

By all accounts, Tyra enjoyed a happy, family-oriented childhood where grandparents, great grandparents, and many aunts, uncles, and cousins were a regular part of family reunions and holidays. By her own admission, Tyra was "spoiled rotten" and "Daddy's little girl." If things weren't going her way, all she'd have to do was cry "a couple crocodile tears" and whatever wish she had was "instantly granted." Whatever Tyra wanted, Daddy got for her, regardless of the cost. Her father even became peeved if Tyra looked at price tags, believing that nothing was too expensive for his baby. Tyra hung on his every word —until she was six and her parents divorced. Suddenly, Tyra felt like her Daddy was the bad guy who had betrayed her and her mother.[6]

Although Tyra's older brother Devin teased her relentlessly for her clumsiness and lack of coordination and often played tricks on her that would showcase her klutziness, they developed a close tie during and after her parent's divorce that continues to this day. Tyra later said that no matter how much Devin taunts and teases her, "I know he's got my back. He has defended me to the end when anyone has tried to hurt me. If a boyfriend does me wrong, he's the first one to kick the guy's butt."[7]

Following the divorce, Tyra went from being "Daddy's little girl" to "Mommy's little girl," forging a skin-tight relationship with her mother that also continues today. Tyra considers her mother her closest friend and advisor, but that doesn't mean they don't sometimes fight like cats and dogs, getting in fights that involve a lot of screaming, fighting, and door slamming until one of them calls the other sheepishly to apologize for being a jerk.[8]

TYRA'S LOVE AFFAIR WITH FOOD

Growing up, Tyra also developed what would later become her trademark appreciation for good and abundant food—and to hell with calories! With grandparents from Louisiana and Texas, there was always plenty of rib-sticking soul food around the house—but not that much of it stuck to Tyra's skinny ribs as a kid. A few of Tyra's favorites were fried chicken wings, barbecued ribs, macaroni and cheese, honeyed ham, smothered pork chops, and candied yams. To this day, Tyra still celebrates important events by sitting down to a good meal, and she isn't afraid to let the world know she enjoys eating. In the event she gained a few extra pounds around her butt and no longer fit into her swimsuit, she simply told the photographers to "Kiss my fat ass!"[9]

Despite the divorce and brotherly taunting, Tyra never forgot her happy, privileged childhood. When she became a supermodel, her fond memories of growing up in Inglewood motivated her to use her fame and fortune to find ways to help less fortunate children by creating scholarships, foundations, and even a summer camp for disadvantaged teenage girls with low self-esteem—something Tyra had plenty of experience with as a teenage girl herself.[10]

A DIVIDE IN THE FAMILY

But not everything was hunky dory in the Banks household. When Tyra was six and Devin was eleven, their parents decided to divorce, shocking Tyra to the tips of her toes. Although she later said she was too young to feel hurt or scared, at the time, she fantasized about doing whatever she could do to get her parents back together again. Fortunately, her parents made a concerted effort to minimize the disruptions to ensure their children continued to enjoy a happy and stable family life.

When her parents divorced, Tyra continued to attend the International Children's School in Los Angeles, a private elementary school that gave her the individual attention and nurturing she needed and helped her maintain the same daily schedule she had always had. Maybe Daddy was no longer living with Mommy, but some things were the same as ever. Tyra still wore the same school uniform every day—a blue jumper with a red and white striped belt. She stayed with her mother in the Inglewood apartment, and her father moved to a house close by, an arrangement that Tyra quickly sized up as being the best of both worlds. "I had it made!" she said in her self-help book for young girls and teens, *Tyra's Beauty Inside & Out*. She got twice the presents she would have received had her parents remained married as well as the chance to celebrate two birthday parties, two Christmases, and so on. "I got twice as many presents and love," she says in her book.[11]

This is not to say that being torn between two households and parents was a piece of cake for Tyra. She later said her parents' divorce taught her the importance of being honest, direct, and maintaining open communication—the very same qualities she tapped into later to become the host of *America's Next Top Model* and *The Tyra Banks Show*. Over time, Tyra began to see that everyone in the family was a lot better off with their new living arrangement. "We were all happier and healthier now that they were living without the marital discord that had precipitated the breakup," she said.

TYRA'S LACK OF FASHION SENSE

Sometimes the smallest things that happen to you growing up turn out to have a lasting effect on you as an adult—in good ways and bad. For Tyra, one of those small things was the fact that she had to wear a uniform to school every day instead of dressing up like girls who went to public school. Later, when Tyra became a TV host, she admitted that because she had grown up wearing a uniform, she had never had the chance to develop her own sense of style or fashion. In fact, when it came to figuring out what to wear at home when she wasn't in front of the camera, she simply did what came naturally and created another uniform for herself to wear—blue jeans and a white shirt.

Even today, Tyra has a stylist come to her apartment and create outfits for her to wear, claiming that otherwise, she might never get dressed! Even her on-air wardrobe is almost a uniform, featuring form-hugging, low-cut dresses that are mostly within the budget and desires of her audience. At the end of each taping, a photo of Tyra, head to toe, is posted on the show's Web site with links to information on where to purchase whatever she it was she was wearing.[12]

"FROGGY'S" IMPORTANT ROLE MODEL

Like many models who go from ugly duckling to swan, Tyra wasn't born drop-dead gorgeous, nor did her parents tell her she was pretty during her youth. She experienced many of the same problems growing up as other young girls or teens—and several that most never had to deal with. When Tyra was nine years old, out of the blue she developed warts on both of her hands, a disconcerting development that led some classmates to nickname her "Froggy."[13] Although her parents assured her that the warts would eventually disappear, when weeks went by and her hands were still speckled with warts, Tyra, showing the fortitude that would later become her trademark, decided to take matters into her own hands by wearing gloves—even in 100 degree temperatures—and when the weather cooled down, by hiding her hands in her pockets. After enduring months of teasing, her father finally agreed to take her to a dermatologist, who froze the warts off and left her with smooth hands. Because of her classmates' teasing, Tyra felt self-conscious about her skin until her Aunt Sharon stepped in and gave her an important beauty tip that Tyra took to heart and has never forgotten—she even repeated it to one of her judges on *America's Next Top Model* who once complained that one of the contestants should be axed because her feet were too big![14]

"Aunt Sharon convinced me the warts weren't my fault, so I shouldn't waste time worrying about them," she told *Us* magazine. "She encouraged me to expend that energy taking care of things I did have control over, like keeping my skin healthy and soft. Aunt Sharon believes the body only gives as good as it gets, so she taught me that keeping the skin in good shape should be a natural extension of my health care routine. Those helpful hints really came in handy with my first *Sports Illustrated* swimsuit issue." Tyra says because of her aunt's advice, she was able to establish a tried-and-true regimen that left her with flawless skin, and which also turned her into a popular model for advertisements and magazine covers because advertisers didn't have to spend a ton of money airbrushing her photos.[15]

Tyra also learned at the tender age of six about the importance of pearly whites, an attribute that would also help pave her way to super-modeldom. (A model with yellow buck teeth? Not on this planet.) On her first visit to the dentist, she had eight cavities, which the "children's dentist" proceeded to fill without using Novocain to numb the pain. Although Tyra had to wear braces as a young teen to straighten her crooked teeth, she took great pains to establish habits that would ensure she'd never have to get near that dentist again.[16]

SHAPING UP INSIDE AND OUT

From the time she was seven, Tyra was also taught the importance of regular exercise in helping develop confidence and perseverance—both crucial skills for budding supermodels. Her mother worked out to exercise videos with friends, performing what Tyra called "nonstop sit-ups" to maintain her figure and urging the friends she worked out with to keep going, even if they were tired or sore. The result, according to Tyra, was a figure "that could put Demi Moore to shame."[17] It wasn't long before Tyra, during her early teenage years, was joining her mother and friends in working out. Eventually, Tyra got bored doing leg lifts and sit-ups and began casting around for a more exciting role model than her mother. When she saw Janet Jackson in her "If" video, she knew she had found her exercise mama. "Damn, I want my body to look like that!" Tyra later told *Us* magazine, adding that wanting to be healthy and fit had absolutely nothing to do with it—she just wanted abs and a butt like Janet's.[18] In an effort to transform herself into a Janet Jackson clone, Tyra worked out in the gym for a couple of weeks and every day would run home, strip down naked in front of the mirror, and pray to see Janet's abs staring back at her. But all she'd see was Tyra's same old stomach. And since she didn't see any new bulging muscles, she said to herself, "What's the point? It's not worth it."[19]

Later, when Tyra achieved supermodel fame, she looked back on her teenage workout goals with Janet and understood why she had given up so fast—they were far too unrealistic and unachievable. Now that she had to maintain a bodacious bod for modeling, she decided to create a workout that would sculpt her without making her fall asleep on the treadmill. Tyra took her exercise regime to the great outdoors, running in the mornings when there were few people around on the streets to race after her hounding her for her autograph. Her three-mile runs took her along the beach, or through grassy parks, and when she really wanted to work up a sweat, she ran up and down outdoor stairs that are found all over Los Angeles and the beach cities. Today, Tyra says working out has made an incredible difference in her overall outlook on life. It's given her incredible energy that lasts the rest of the day, and the benefits of working out have spilled over into her work life as well by helping her understand the importance of determination and "stick-to-it-ive-ness." Today, when she looks in the mirror, Tyra says she's not looking for bulging muscles. "I just admire my progress," she says. "I've learned to work within my own pace. When I see how far I've come, I know that my persistence is paying off and that makes me feel darn good."[20]

TYRA JUST SAYS NO

As a child, Tyra also learned some life-preserving health lessons that would serve her well as a supermodel, including the dangers of smoking. When she was six, she was playing hide-and-seek with a friend when she stumbled upon a cigarette burning in an ash tray. Curious, Tyra picked up the cigarette, inhaled deeply, and filled her mouth with smoke. Not realizing she was supposed to exhale the smoke, she swallowed it instead and started coughing and gagging as the smoke scorched her throat and chest. After that incident, Tyra said she was "totally turned off of cigarettes." Tyra's views on smoking were solidified when her beloved grandmother, Florine London, died at age 50 from lung cancer, having smoked since she was 13 years old. Because Tyra saw "up close" what habitual smoking could lead to, she vowed she would never promote smoking or tobacco. True to her word, Tyra has refused all offers to model for cigarette ads. Unlike many famous supermodels and celebrities who use smoking to dull their appetite and stay thin, Tyra continues to speak out against smoking to anyone who will listen, including the millions of fans who watch her television shows.[21]

Smoking wasn't the only societal vice Tyra decided to pass on at a young age—and still passes on as a famous adult. When she was 13, she also decided to "just say no" to alcohol after a friend offered her a taste of a peach wine cooler. Tyra took a sip and knew immediately that alcohol was not her thing, especially since she had watched her friend drink to the point of unconsciousness. In an industry rife with drinking, Tyra's non-drinking ways have made her stand out from the hoards of Hollywood celebs who think nothing of getting plastered the minute the camera points in another direction (or, sometimes, even when the camera is pointed at them!).[22] In fact, Tyra says the only people who object to her not drinking are other people. "It sure seems to make other people feel uneasy," she says. Whenever she refused a drink, Tyra says she'd get "strange looks, as if to say, 'Who is she trying to impress?'" But after running into the same people over and over again in all kinds of social settings, Tyra says her friends and colleagues have become accustomed to "passing me a virgin pina colada. People often tell me they want to be the first ones to see me drunk, and my response is always the same: It's not gonna happen!"[23]

Tyra has the same attitude towards drugs, which were instilled in her by her mother, a "hippie chick" whose friends called her a square for not giving in to peer pressure to get high. Even without drugs, Tyra says her mother was still the life of the party—so much so that people often asked if they could have whatever she was on. Like mother, like daughter. Tyra says when she's at a party with friends, she's so "pumped up" that people think she's actually on something. When people ask if they can have what she's drinking (smoking or snorting), she tells them, "I'm flying on a natural high!"[24]

EARLY LESSONS IN FINANCE

After Tyra's parents divorced, Tyra and Devin lived with their mother in a one-bedroom apartment in Inglewood, an experience that taught her the importance of being frugal. By the time Tyra was 19 years old, she had saved $10,000, which her mother, Carolyn, who managed her for the first seven years of her career, from the time she was in Paris, placed with a Merrill Lynch firm. (Tyra has remained with the unnamed adviser ever since.)

Tyra took her mother's advice on frugality to heart. Today, even though she has buckets of money—*Fortune* magazine just named her the top earning female entertainer with an annual income of $28 million in 2008—Tyra continues to be a penny pincher. "I still have a poverty demon," she admitted long after her name became a household word. "I'll ask my accountant if I can afford something, and he'll say, 'What are you talking about? Of course you can.' "

When Tyra formed her own production company, originally named Ty Girl Corporation, she later decided to rename it Bankable Productions after her frugal business sense. The name proved to be prophetic. "So far, my production company has been very bankable."[25]

A NEW FATHER IN THE FAMILY

In 1983, Tyra's mother announced she was getting remarried to Clifford Johnson, Jr., a high school graphics arts teacher. Tyra worried that her mother had cast her aside and betrayed her and felt that her stepfather would take her mother away from her. Tyra attempted to put her feelings aside for her mother's sake. "Instead of whining, sulking, and throwing a tantrum, I put a smile on my face and wished my mom the best of luck." But despite her show of acceptance, Tyra was conflicted about her stepfather, a strict disciplinarian who expected Tyra and Devin to follow his orders without question. For instance, if she left her clothing on the bedroom floor, her stepfather would wake her up and demand that she put them away. If she neglected to do the dishes to his satisfaction, he make her do them again. Compared to her mother's relaxed attitude toward child-raising, Tyra felt Clifford was a tyrant and bully, and resented his strictness. Her resentment blinded her to his many positive qualities, which included always being there for her and his immense talent as an artist.

Over time, however, Tyra began to see her stepfather as an individual and learned to communicate with and care for him. "I had to allow myself to meet my stepfather halfway," she says in her book. "Just that little step took our relationship forward by leaps and bounds."[26] Tyra says thanks to her stepdad, today she can clean a house, cook a meal, and iron clothes "much better than most women of my generation."[27]

PRETEEN GROWING PAINS

Before turning 12, Tyra entered an awkward stage which she refers to as a time she would never want to relive, but which actually was the beginning of the "model" physique she later became famous for. Over a period of three months, Tyra grew three inches and lost 20 pounds. At 5′ 9″ and a rail-thin 98 pounds, Tyra towered over most of her friends and even her teachers. But, of course, at age 12, no one (at least back in those days) wanted to have the body of a supermodel. They just wanted to be the same size as everyone else!

Concerned that Tyra might have a medical disorder, her mother took her to see several doctors, all of whom pronounced her healthy as a horse and assured her she would eventually gain weight. Meanwhile, her classmates taunted her with names like "Olive Oyl" and "Lightbulb" because her head seemed to be too large for her ultra-thin body. Tyra recalls in her book that classmates made unkind comments such as, "Gosh, she's so skinny she'd blow away if a big wind came along," and "Quick, somebody give her a pork chop." Tyra felt like such a freak and like her body had betrayed her that she slowly reverted into herself, going from a former extrovert and class clown to a shy, withdrawn introvert who spent much of her time locked in her room.[28]

Tyra said she was so uncomfortable with her skinny body that she did some pretty unhealthy things to attempt to gain weight, including stuffing herself with artery-clogging, fattening foods.[29]

JUST THE GIRLS

In 1984, Tyra, then 10 years old, graduated from elementary school and entered John Burroughs Middle School in Los Angeles. Having become accustomed to small classes and the intimate environment at her private elementary school, she found the public middle school's expansive campus intimidating and overwhelming. In 1987, she entered the all-girls Immaculate Heart Middle and High School, a prestigious Catholic school in the Los Feliz section of Los Angeles.[30]

At first, Tyra wasn't sure she would enjoy going to school with just girls—especially after her grade school experience with catty class-mates who teased her about her height and weight. But she soon found the absence of males to be a definite asset because it allowed the studi-ous and bookish Tyra to focus on her studies so she could get straight A's and one day be a vet, instead of worrying about "looking cute" or spending hours styling her hair or makeup to impress the guys. The school also gave Tyra more opportunities to hold leadership positions in student government and sports and showed her that young girls could be as strong and independent as boys—again, lessons she'd later need in the cutthroat world of supermodeling where most of the rules were made by men who didn't have to starve themselves to fit into size 0 jeans.[31]

Meanwhile, Tyra remained "Olive Oyl" stick-thin as she moved into her teens, claiming all the popular girls at her school started to develop breasts and hips but that her body just stayed the same—straight and narrow. However, the teasing eventually stopped, and Tyra came out of her closet and began to make friends, even though she still wasn't thrilled with her body. "I don't think I felt good about my figure until I turned 17, when I began to gain weight and actually started developing some curves," says Tyra.

As luck would have it—or not!—Tyra began gaining just as her modeling career began taking off—and just when a few extra pounds here or there could be professional suicide. But even Tyra's horrific experience as "Olive Oyl" served her well as a supermodel. Because she had always despised her stick-thin figure and longed for curves, by the time she became a supermodel, she had no desire to emulate the ultra-thin, anorexic-looking models, and she refused to deny herself the foods she loved, including french fries and ice cream. "I don't starve myself," she tells readers in her book. "I don't really diet at all. Letting go a little is my way of saying to other women, 'Don't let fash-ion make you insecure.'"[32]

Her attitude toward the fashion industry extended to the media when, many years later, Tyra's dimensions—bigger than they had ever been in her runway days, caught the attention of the media, who criti-cized her for having the nerve to gain weight! Her response to the media has become something of a battle-cry to women the world over who are picked on for being too chubby: "Kiss my fat ass!"

Tyra's towering height also set her apart from the pack at an age when all she wanted to do was fit in. During high school, Tyra kept growing taller, an attribute the school's sports coaches found encouraging until they saw her play. Tyra says she was so clumsy and uncoordinated that she eventually became the official bench-warmer. When the volleyball coach finally agreed to let her play a match, she sprained her forearm. When Tyra made the basketball team, she says she "couldn't shoot to save my life. So, unless we were way ahead or hopelessly behind, I didn't see much court time."[33]

Years later, because of her height Tyra was approached by Hollywood producers to play a woman who ran track for a college team for the movie, *Higher Learning*. Tyra trained with a top coach from UCLA who had also won an Olympic gold medal in track. While she eventually got the hang of running, Tyra never quite mastered the hurdles, initially tripping and falling facedown on the ground. But her coach insisted she keep trying, and Tyra managed to make it over five more hurdles. Even though the producer decided to use a body double for the hurdling shots lest Tyra fall and bite the dust, Tyra considered it a "major achievement to have reached a place I couldn't imagine being only three weeks before."[34]

FUMBLES IN TEENAGE LOVE

If Tyra had trouble scoring on the playing field, as a teenager, she wasn't much more successful at scoring great dates, as she relates in her book, *Tyra's Beauty Inside & Out*. A few days after her 16th birthday, she worked up the courage to ask out an "older man" in the neighborhood whom she had been admiring from a distance. His name was Derek, and he was on the local hockey team and a freshman in college. Tyra says with all that going for him, she just assumed she was going out with a "superfine college man." Derek took her to see the movie, *The Little Mermaid*, which Tyra thought was innocent enough. But ten minutes into the movie, Derek started making suggestive comments about what a great body the mermaid had. Tyra says in her mind she was thinking, "Hello—reality check! She's a cartoon!" Despite his ignorant comments and behavior, Tyra went out with him again and again, until he took her to see the movie, *Beauty and the Beast*. "When he started going on about how sexy Belle was, then I knew it was time to move on," she said.

On another occasion, Tyra went to pick up her date at his house, only to find him hanging out with six of his rowdy buddies, all of whom told Tyra how lucky she was to be going out with him. Tyra bolted for her car and listened to her car radio for 45 minutes while her date spent 45 minutes showering and primping for the date. Obviously, that relationship didn't last long, either—although that guy must be pretty embarrassed today that he blew it big time with a girl who would go on to become a supermodel and TV star.[35]

In her book, Tyra also relates her dismal experiences with guys who did nothing but "talk about their resumes and how many famous Hollywood actresses they'd 'done,' " and with men who "spent the entire time looking at themselves in the mirrored wall behind him." Despite her early dating disasters—not to mention her more recent fiascos (many a magazine article has quoted Tyra on how lonely and/ or brokenhearted she is)—Tyra said she's still willing to put herself out there. "I'm not about to let a few trifling guys spoil it for me. You've got to kiss a lot of frogs before you find a prince," she says in her book.[36]

TYRA DISCOVERS FASHION

As Tyra got more comfortable at Immaculate Heart High School and made some supportive new friends, she began to come out of her shell. Although she was still reed-thin, her mother and friends taught her to look at the bright side of her physique: She had more clothing options than someone who was short and fat. With some encouragement from Carolyn and a close friend, Khefri Riley, Tyra began developing her own sense of style. Of course, it was pretty difficult to make her school uniform stylish—Tyra said she had the big choice of choosing between two skirts, either gray wool in winter or yellow cotton in summer, alternating between blue, yellow, or white shirt collars, and wearing penny loafers or oxfords—not exactly the stuff of fashion magazines. But practice makes perfect, or so they say. During her high school years, Tyra became so used to the school board dictating what she could wear that she ended up creating a weekend uniform for her-self to wear, which was plain old jeans and a white T-shirt.[37]

Khefri, Tyra's friend, who was really into fashion, persuaded Tyra that she was very attractive, especially when she made some effort to dress up. Khefri talked Tyra into going shopping with her at the local thrift stores, where they rooted through the racks for hours finding inexpensive items of clothing to create eclectic wardrobes. Tyra's mother, a photographer with an eye for line and proportions, also stepped in, sensing a chance to ignite her daughter's interest in fash-ion. When Tyra found something she liked, her mother would find something similar and less expensive and buy it for her, then photo-graph Tyra in her outfit (good practice for what would later become Tyra's way of earning a living!). Her mother even brought in a seam-stress to recreate an expensive prom dress Tyra had seen in a store.[38] Once Tyra got into the flow, nothing stopped her. She and her friend would also raid Thrifty's for cheap makeup, then go home and experi-ment with it. "We thought we were so cool," Tyra later told *People* magazine.[39]

"YOU OUGHT TO BE A MODEL"

Khefri, who had already signed with a modeling agency, urged Tyra to give modeling a try, even though it was something Tyra had never really considered. Her real childhood dream was to be a veterinarian (with the beautiful nom de vet of "Stephanie Clifton").[40]

"I said, 'What?'" Tyra recalled. "I was very skinny and kind of awk-ward. I told my mama, and because she was a photographer, we started doing some test shots."[41] Finally, after a year of badgering her friend, in 1989 Tyra relented and agreed to look for an agency. Her first model-ing job was for a magazine called *Black Collegiate*. Tyra said she was "so excited because there was a little picture of me on the cover, above the title."[42]

But Tyra's initial optimism soon turned to disappointment as one agency after another turned her down. One agency looked at her pho-tos for less than a minute before doing so. "It's definitely not all fun and games, especially for models of color," said Tyra. After stopping at Khefri's agency, who gave her the once over and told her she didn't have the look they wanted at the time, she went to a second agency, who said they had enough girls already who looked like her. The next agency said her features were too ethnic, and the next one said they already had a black girl and didn't have the time, energy, or room for another. According to Tyra, they took her photos to another room and returned in less than one minute and said, "Thanks, but no thanks." says Tyra.[43]

"The market for black models was not very good," recalls Tyra's mother, Carolyn, who shot Tyra's portfolio and accompanied her on interviews. "They would say, 'we have this many black girls already.' " Her looks, Tyra was told, were "too ethnic."[44]

Discouraged, Tyra decided to try one more agency before calling it quits. She walked in, handed her photos to the secretary, and waited for what seemed like hours. Finally, one of the agents came to the front office to meet her. She sat down in front of Tyra and said, "Well, Tyra, I see that you have some potential. But I'm only going to have you do runway shows, because I don't feel that the camera likes your face."[45] Despite the agency's lack of enthusiasm, Tyra signed with L.A. Models, her parents and brother both very supportive as she took her first career step,[46]

After signing with the agency, Tyra began juggling schoolwork and small modeling jobs. Because she took both very seriously, neither one suffered. In fact, Tyra, ever the studious student, simply studied for the different aspects of modeling as she would study for a class, doing photos sessions and walking until she felt confident enough to go on a runway. She also learned to do her own makeup so she wouldn't have to depend on makeup arts and studied her face in the mirror so she wouldn't miss anything or take anything for granted.[47]

In 1990, Tyra switched to another modeling agency, Elite Model Management, where she felt more accepted, if not exactly encouraged. She also continued to work hard on her studies, having changed her mind about being a vet and deciding on a career in film and television production. While she enjoyed the extra money modeling provided during high school, Tyra didn't really think of it as a permanent job or a substitute for her "real life." After taking her college exams, Tyra applied to five different colleges in the Los Angeles area, and was thrilled to be accepted at Loyola Marymount, her first choice.[48]

In the summer of 1991, Tyra, still planning to go to Loyola Mary-mount University in the fall, was booked for a shoot with *Seventeen* magazine. "I vividly remember walking into my modeling agency all happy and excited, but, of course, someone had to break the mood," says Tyra. The receptionist called her over and said, "Tyra, honey, you better wipe that cheesy grin off your face. I'll let you know that black models don't have a chance at making it in this industry. So I suggest you come off that cloud you're floating on and learn how to type. Because next year, you'll probably be applying for my job."

Tyra says had she listened to her, she probably would have thrown in the towel right then and there. "But I stayed strong and stuck with it. I don't know where that woman is today, but I'm sure she's eating her words."[49]

That August, a month before Tyra was supposed to start college, a French modeling agent scouting for talent in LA, offered her an imme-diate chance to model at the couture shows in Paris. Tyra accepted, and the rest is history. Within a few weeks after arriving in Paris, Tyra had accumulated a record 25 bookings and had begun attracting the notice of other supermodels in Paris. One of them, Naomi Campbell, another black supermodel, was so threatened by Tyra's immediate suc-cess that she had her banned from modeling in a Chanel show. But other supermodels were quick to come to Tyra's defense, cheering the young Tyra on and giving her the support and encouragement she needed to avoid feeling discouraged and defeated by Naomi. "That girl is a live wire," fellow supermodel Niki Taylor told *People*. "She can work a runway like you would not believe."[50]

NOTES

1. Lila Chase, *Totally Tyra: An Unauthorized Biography* (New York: Penguin Group, 2006), 1.

2. Pam Levin, *Tyra Banks* (Philadelphia: Chelsea House Publish-ers, 2000), 23.

3. Ibid., 23–24.

4. David Frum, *How We Got Here: The '70s* (New York: Basic Books, 2000), 292–93.

5. Ibid.

6. Tyra Banks, *Tyra's Beauty Inside & Out* (New York: Harper Collins, 1998), 174.

7. Ibid., 171.

8. Ibid.

9. Levin, *Tyra Banks*, 24.

10. Levin, *Tyra Banks*, 26.

11. Banks, *Tyra's Beauty Inside & Out*, 170.

12. "Tyra Banks' Biggest Modeling Struggle," *Us*, May 29, 2008, www.usmagazine.com/tyra-banks-biggest-modeling-struggle-i-was-black-and-curvy.

13. Levin, *Tyra Banks*, 13.

14. Banks, *Tyra's Beauty Inside & Out*, 29.

15. Ibid., 19.

16. Ibid., 28.

17. Ibid., 29.

18. Ibid., 89.

19. Ibid.

20. Ibid.

21. Ibid., 28–29.

22. Ibid., 36.

23. Ibid.

24. Ibid.

25. Ibid., 170.

26. Ibid.

27. Quoted in Levin, *Tyra Banks*, 200.

28. Banks, *Tyra's Beauty Inside & Out*, 170.

29. Levin, *Tyra Banks*, 34.

30. Banks, *Tyra's Beauty Inside & Out*, 84.

31. Levin, *Tyra Banks*, 33.

32. Banks, *Tyra's Beauty Inside & Out*, 84.

33. Ibid., 32.

34. Ibid., 97.

35. Ibid., 139–40.

36. Ibid., 107.

37. Ibid.

38. Levin, *Tyra Banks*, 38.

39. Quoted in Tom Gliatto, "Tyrasaurus," *People*, April 11, 1994, www.people.com/people/archive/article/0,,20107829,00.html (accessed May 13, 2009).

40. Ibid.

41. Quoted by Lynn Hirschberg, "Banksable," *New York Times Magazine*, June 1, 2008, www.nytimes.com/2008/06/01/magazine/01tyra-t.html.

42. Tyra Banks, "An Empire Behind the Scenes," *Newsweek*, October 13, 2008, www.newsweek.com/id/162338 (accessed May 13, 2009).

43. Banks, *Tyra's Beauty Inside & Out*, 165–66.

44. Quoted in Gliatto, "Tyrasaurus."

45. Levin, *Tyra Banks*, 39.

46. Gliatto, "Tyrasaurus."

47. Levin, *Tyra Banks*, 40.

48. Ibid.

49. Banks, *Tyra's Beauty Inside & Out*, 167.

50. Quoted in Gliatto, "Tyrasaurus."

Chapter 2

THE ACCIDENTAL SUPERMODEL

The year 1991 was a life-changing one for 17-year-old Tyra Banks. She would set out on a course that would lead to her becoming one of the world's top supermodels as well as an internationally renowned TV host and producer.

It had all started in the summer of 1990. Still a high school senior and planning to enroll at Loyola Marymount University in the fall, Tyra was selected by *Seventeen* magazine to be photographed for its March 1991 issue. L.A. Models, Tyra's agent at the time, had been contacted by the magazine and the agency had sent them some photos of Tyra. The editors were very impressed by the tall, beautiful girl who appeared to be having such a great time in front of the camera. They hired Tyra on the spot and sent their crew to Los Angeles to meet her and photograph her for the upcoming issue.[1]

Although Tyra was not aware of it at the time, the *Seventeen* photos were just the start of a long career in front of the camera. Only two weeks before she was to start college, her plans were abruptly interrupted when her new agency, Elite Model Management, introduced her to a representative from a French modeling agency The agency wanted to sponsor Tyra for a year to model at the haute couture shows in Paris, participate in the fall/winter 1991 season, and remain in Paris for the 1991 spring/summer shows. Too excited to believe her luck,

Tyra accepted the offer to live and work in the fashion capital of the world for a year, putting her studies on hold for a year after Loyola Marymount gave her a year's deferment.[2]

The chance to work the runway shows in Paris, where fashion is taken extremely seriously, is the lifelong dream of every model on earth. But it also entailed a great deal of work, which Tyra was quick to grasp. Her mother warned her that if she wanted to be a model, she had to study hard because modeling was a real job.

PRACTICING HER RUNWAY STRUT

Taking her advice to heart, Tyra prepared for her trip to Paris by watching MTV's *House of Style*, with Cindy Crawford, over and over again. Tyra says she especially admired the way Cindy parlayed her modeling career into one that reached into many different areas—information she filed for later use. Tyra also rented videotapes from the library of the Fashion Design Institute to practice walking correctly on the runway, "putting on my mother's robes and high heels and walking up and down the living room before I went to Paris."[3]

At first, Tyra's model strut was "lame, lame, lame," she recalled to *People* magazine. My ankles would shake and I would bend my knees and stick my lips out," she said, adding that the first time she walked down a runway in Los Angeles, "I was horrible. I was walking with my lips stuck out 'cause I thought it was sexy."[4]

Runway stance aside, one of the most important things Tyra needed for her modeling career was a professional photo portfolio to show to designers and print agencies in Paris. Lucky for her, she had just the mother for the job! Using her photography background and expertise, Carolyn began photographing her daughter in a variety of poses for the portfolio, and managed to capture Tyra's beauty, charisma, and versatility.[5] "My mom was a medical photographer. After hours, she would sometimes take pictures of me and my brother in her studio. When I look at those pictures, I realize I am posing. I have my hand on my chin and I'm looking right at the camera. It's so funny that the little [girl in the photo] was a supermodel in the making."[6]

PARIS BOUND

Before she knew it, September had rolled around and Tyra was en route to Paris, traveling on a plane without a chaperone for the first time in her life. After two weeks in Paris, she got her first magazine cover when the French magazine, *20 Ans* ("Twenty Years," for twenty-year-olds) invited her to do a shoot. The magazine donned Tyra in a black-trimmed red jacket and pants and shot her under bright studio lights, presenting an image of both innocence and allure to the world.[7]

Tyra's look captivated the world as well as major fashion houses. Within one week, she landed spots on the runway at 25 different fashion shows, including the legendary Yves Saint Laurent, Oscar de la Renta, Chanel, Giorgio Armani, and Karl Lagerfield. Her smile and exuberance delighted the audiences as she strode down the aisle in everything from elegant suits to fluffy confections.[8]

Despite her months of practicing back home in Los Angeles, on a real runway Tyra's professional catwalk was anything but ordinary. More of an animated bounce than a walk, Tyra said that on the runway, "I was the only one of the girls who didn't walk like a soldier." Tyra's unusual catwalk, while undoubtedly the product of inexperience, actually managed to set her apart from the pack—which in the modeling biz is a good thing. "The first time I did his show, Todd Oldham told me to 'work it,' but he didn't know I would really 'work it,'" she recalls. Not only did the crowd go wild for Tyra, but Oldham credits her catwalk style to some animal instinct. "She reminds me of a gazelle. She was just born with grace."[9] Said Bethann Hardison, president of a management company for models and a former runway model herself, when watching Tyra model in Paris, "She works the runway like the black beauties from the 1970s—the Pat Clevelands, the Alva Chins, the Billie Blairs, or the black models you see in church fashion shows. Tyra knows her role. She entertains, but at the same time, she's there to sell. And she does just that."[10]

TYRA'S TROUBLED TIMES IN PARIS

Despite her instant success on the catwalk, Tyra was having difficulty adjusting to everyday life in Paris. While she found the city fascinating and spent hours walking the streets absorbing the people, language, and culture, she was also very lonely and homesick—not to mention starving for her favorite American foods. When asked years later about how she felt as a young model in Paris, Tyra recalled that she was "lonely in Paris in a model's apartment the size of a breadbox and extremely homesick with no friends or family around." Tyra overcame her longing for home by eating her way through all of the American fast-food restaurants in Paris, from McDonalds and Burger King to Haagen-Dazs, and she also begged her mother to send her care packages of snacks from home. Unfortunately, Tyra's unhealthy diet of "sandwich cookies for breakfast, peanut brittle for lunch and caramel corn for dinner" zapped her of her energy, and she nearly fainted on the runway.[11] "Paris was weird and confusing for me. I felt overwhelmed by all that was happening," Tyra later recalled. "I was 17, and I didn't know how to take care of myself. I asked my mom to send care packages of Fiddle Faddle and Oreos. I ended up eating them for breakfast, lunch and dinner. So I got sick. When my mom came to visit me, she saw all of that and refused to send me any more packages. She taught me how to shop and cook."[12]

On the social level, Tyra was becoming something of an oddball and outcast, preferring to remain by herself rather than socialize with the other models. Uninterested in Paris nightlife or the party scene, she preferred visiting museums and shopping in Paris' small grocery stores, butcher shops, and renowned bakeries, where she loved inhaling the smells of fresh baked goods in the ovens. Talking with tourists at sidewalk cafes and practicing her French with shop owners also helped fill the human void.

In time, Tyra discovered she enjoyed her new independence. When her mother came to visit her for the first time, she was struck by how her daughter had learned to get around on her own. Tyra later said her early experiences in Paris made her aware of her true inner strengths and helped hone her survival skills in the modeling industry, which was renowned for its big egos and even bigger fangs.[13]

RUNWAY RIVAL

Tyra's early days in the modeling business were difficult for her in another sense as well. Subtle racism within the industry was partly responsible; from the start, Tyra was called the "new Naomi Campbell," in comparison to the more experienced supermodel who had been the star woman of color on the runways for some years. Campbell, known for her diva-like behavior, was incensed, and managed to get Tyra barred from appearing in a Chanel show after refusing to speak to her on several other occasions.[14]

"No model should have to endure what I went through at 17," Tyra told *People* in 1994. "It's very sad that the fashion business and press can't accept that there can be more than one reigning black supermodel at a time. I have 20 magazine covers in Europe and only a few in America—*Essence* for one."[15]

And if her personal habits caused her to become an oddball and outcast among the other models, that was just tough, she told *Details* magazine in 1997 "I didn't drink, I didn't smoke, I didn't do drugs or anything like that in high school, so when I started modeling, I was just the same person," she said. "I didn't speak the language, and I'm not very social. I tend to be by myself, so I didn't have a lot of friends. I'd go to the movies by myself. And I was pretty lonely, because a lot of models like to party and drink and hang out and I wasn't into that."[16] Fortunately, Tyra's mother had given her a strong work ethic—a combination of being professional, punctual, and poised, that helped Tyra weather the bumps in Paris and keep things in perspective. But as Tyra's modeling career moved into high gear, it was clear to everyone that she needed a full-time manager. Tyra knew exactly who fit the bill for the job. Fortunately, it was a person who couldn't say no.

DON'T BELIEVE THE HYPE

About a year after her stunning modeling debut, Tyra called her mother, Carolyn, and begged her to come to Paris and be her manager. Carolyn was scared, but decided it was in Tyra's best interest to have her there. "Tyra's modeling agency was very concerned about [Tyra's] success happening so rapidly," Carolyn later told the *San Jose Mercury News.* "They wanted me to come there so that they could school me about the industry and although I had a full-time job, I took vacation and went. It was the scariest thing I have ever done, but it was the best thing I could have done. It gave her the freedom to concentrate on her work."[17]

Another lesson Carolyn taught Tyra early in her career in Paris was not to believe the hype printed about her in the media—a piece of advice that has helped keep Tyra's head on straight later in her career, when the kudos began coming in fast and furious from magazines around the world. She also told her young daughter to enjoy the ride while it lasted, because success is often fleeting. "My mother told me not to believe the hype; that these people aren't really loving Tyra," she told the *Mercury News*. "It's just the girl in the pictures they are loving. Mom told me years ago, and I know that it's true, that the phone may be ringing today, but it can stop ringing tomorrow, and that has kept me grounded from the beginning."[18]

Sam Fine, an internationally known makeup artist who worked with Tyra, told *Details* magazine that Tyra had apparently taken her mother's advice to heart and used it well. "Tyra's approach to the modeling industry has always been about understanding the business and making it work for her. She knows this is a business; she is never fooled by the glamour and phoniness. She knows that it's about the lights, the makeup and the clothes, and she is not so caught up in herself."[19]

Unlike many young supermodels, Tyra was already busy making plans for what she would do with her life after she stopped modeling, a career she knew she didn't want to be in forever. In fact, after a year on the catwalk, Tyra had already had her fill of backstage jealousy, cliques, and insecurities, and had decided she didn't want to end her career by being a pretty face on the runway. Her long-range goal—and one that has followed her throughout her career, was to find a way to use her fame and fortune to help less fortunate women reach their dreams and goals.

TYRA COMES HOME

By the time Tyra came home from Paris in October 1992, her success on the Paris runway had spread her name throughout the fashion world, and she had also matured and become her own person. But her immediate goals had nothing to do with high fashion or runways. She wanted to create a scholarship at her former high school for young African American women, and she also wanted to create her own corporation.

Tyra hadn't yet turned 19 when she decided to found the Tyra Banks Scholarship for African American girls at Immaculate Heart High School. In 1993, a year later, she established Ty Girl Corporation, which she later named Bankable, Inc. Tyra's new career soon became a family affair, with Tyra's mother becoming her manager and her father tapped to handle Tyra's growing fortune and ever-more-complicated financial affairs. Tyra also hired a cousin to handle the avalanche of fan mail she was getting from young girls and teens.[20]

STILL THE SAME GOOFY TYRA

While success had certainly given Tyra fame and fortune, those close to her maintained that she was still the same down-to-earth girl. Tyra's overnight success didn't turn her into a mega-spending diva, as it had done with so many other young supermodels and celebrities. She didn't go out and buy a palatial mansion in Beverly Hills or embark on jet-setting vacations to the South of France. In fact, in 1994, two years after she had returned to Paris, Tyra was still living with her mother and stepfather and had camped out in her old bedroom surrounded by her stuffed animals! She retained close ties to her biological father, Douglas Banks, a computer consultant who lived nearby, and also corresponded regularly with her brother, Devin, who by then was an Air Force paramedic stationed in Okinawa.[21]

Her mother, Carolyn, told *People* magazine that Tyra "tended not to comb [her] hair or wear makeup on off days," and said in real life, "Tyra is just real goofy, not at all like the sexy model that slithers along the runways." "I try, at least on my answering machine" (to sound sexy) Tyra joked to *People*. "I try lowering my voice and talking sexy, but it just doesn't work."[22]

Down-home girl aside, it soon became clear that Tyra was bound for bigger things than hanging out in her bedroom with her favorite furry friends. No sooner did she settle in at home when offers began pouring in for her to model for magazines. Tyra began jetting around the world, becoming a regular presence in fashion capitals like New York, London, and Rome, and appearing on countless magazine covers, including *Cosmopolitan*, *Vogue*, *Elle*, *Esquire*, and *Harper's Bazaar*. Despite her youthful energy, Tyra found living on the road very lonely. "The endless travel is hard sometimes. Being alone in hotel rooms all over the world can be very lonely—thank God for the telephone!"[23]

GETTING A LITTLE BOOTY

After a year of jet-setting around the globe, Tyra was convinced that her days of catwalking and being a cover girl for women's fashion magazines were coming to a close—and not just because her goals were changing. After years of being a stick—which was well and good for modeling—Tyra was finally gaining weight, which for a supermodel is usually professional suicide.[24]

Even though people were still hiring her, curves and all, Tyra was becoming more and more self-conscious. She wore a size eight, but compared to some of the other less-endowed models in the industry, she was full figured. Even in Paris, her size had made it hard to work with some designers because their clothing was tailored for a size-two or size-four model in mind. "Their attitude was that if you wanted to work for them, you had to be able to fit into their cloths—no ifs, ands, or buts. And since that wasn't my size, I'd lose out on some major jobs," said Tyra.[25] Her modeling agency had even compiled a list titled, "Designers who will not book Tyra because of hips and breasts." As a last resort, Tyra's agency in Paris had begged her mother to put her daughter on a diet. "My mother told me the whole thing as we were walking down the street in Milan," says Tyra. "She said, 'They say you're too curvy. Let's go order pizza.'" The mother and daughter walked into a pizzeria and discussed Tyra's career change. Obviously, her curves were going to dictate a new type of modeling.[26]

As Tyra later told Diane Sawyer on *Good Morning America*, "I used to do *Vogue* and *Harper's Bazaar*. I was seventeen and skinny, but then I was 20, and I got a little booty, you know, things were happening. And I was like, I'm not going to starve myself like I see my colleagues doing, I can't do this."[27] In fact, even at her thinnest, Tyra had always weighed 20 to 30 pounds more than most supermodels, which she had always considered a "positive thing." Unfortunately, the modeling biz didn't agree. "It's so bad that people are saying that's bad."[28]

Fellow black supermodel Veronica Webb later recalled that Tyra had been smart to veer away from runway modeling and sign a contract with Victoria's Secret, pointing out that anyone with a bodacious body like Tyra could make a lot more money modeling a bikini, bra, and panties than modeling clothing on the runway.[29]

THE ALL-AMERICAN BLACK GIRL

While Tyra knew she was a successful model, she never truly identified with the fashion world, claiming that when she had on a $30,000 gown, she almost felt like she was in a Halloween costume. And even when she was booking nonstop shows in Paris, she was never entirely seduced by the high-fashion world. She also never forgot her mother's prophetic words about the fickle nature of the fashion and modeling industry. "My mother would say: 'Remember the girl that was hot last season and isn't here anymore? That's going to be you. You're like an athlete, and they're going to look for the next draft pick. You have to think of the end at the beginning.'"[30] After a few years on the road modeling, Tyra was ready to start thinking about the next stage of her career.

Casting about for a role as a supermodel who had gone on and done bigger and better things, Tyra settled on Cindy Crawford who represented cosmetic and swimsuit calendars, and made even more money than she had as a catwalk model. Cindy had been a high-fashion girl who had successfully segued into being an all-American girl. Tyra realized that no black model had ever attempted to be Cindy Crawford. While supermodels like Iman were intimidating divas, they weren't like, "Hi! Here's a Pepsi!" said Tyra. She decided she wanted to follow in Cindy's path and become the all-American black woman next door.

Instead of bucking the tide or giving up, Tyra decided to take charge of her destiny. Realizing that no black model had ever really succeeded in the commercial world before, she decided to shift her goals away from the runway and do what she called a Cindy Crawford or Claudia Schiffer. "I've always been attracted to models whose careers tapped in[to] the commercial [world], like Cindy Crawford and Claudia Schiffer. Like them, I have a little more meat on my bones. For runway and fashion magazines, they're always looking for the new thing and they kick out the old ones. I just noticed that the commercial market hadn't been tapped by black women before."[31] Tyra asked her agent to start looking for commercial work for her that would accompany her growing bootie. Tyra soon was doing advertisements for Liz Clairborne, Ralph Lauren, Swatch watches, and Pepsi.

COVERGIRL CALLING

In between all the jet-setting to fashion shoots around the world, Tyra got a phone call that would change her destiny. CoverGirl was calling to ask if Tyra would consider being a high-profile model and spokesperson for the company and appear in print and television commercials. Tyra said yes, becoming the third African American woman in the history of CoverGirl to represent the firm. She signed a lucrative but exclusive contract that forbid her from modeling for other similar businesses, but which instantly signaled to the world that she had arrived. Like earlier cover girls Cheryl Tiegs and Christie Brinkley, Tyra's CoverGirl exposure suddenly catapulted her onto the world stage of national television and high-profile fashion magazines, and was an open door to countless other invitations and opportunities. Tyra's idols weren't Naomi Campbell or even Linda Evangelista; they were Claudia Schiffer and Cindy Crawford. They took their name and made it into a business and that's what she wanted to do. The CoverGirl exposure was a real coup for Tyra. Everyone want to look as beautiful as CoverGirl models, and the print and TV ads portrayed her the way Tyra really believed she was—a woman with a wholesome, girl-next-door sexiness. In fact, when GQ magazine interviewed her about her first sexual encounter, Tyra said she couldn't possibly reveal that information because she was a sweet, all-American cover girl.[32]

TYRA'S BIG TV BREAK

Once Tyra became a CoverGirl, her life became one breakthrough after another—but she still felt as if she was operating on too-small of a stage. Tyra had planned on majoring in film before her gig in Paris changed her plans. In fact, she had wanted to be an actress, director, and producer long before she became a supermodel. Tyra felt that acting just came naturally to her. When her mother's friends used to come over for the holidays, she'd get her cousins and friends together, choreograph dances, and be the lead singer and perform for them.[33]

On another level, Tyra had also grown weary of the many prejudices she encountered in the modeling business, battling people who told her she couldn't do this or that because she was black. Tyra said the constant "you can't's" never made her bitter, but they did make her anxious to prove them all wrong![34]

Tyra began looking for ways to break into the movie business. Fortunately, she didn't have to wait long, Her first big break came in 1994 when she landed a recurring role in the popular sitcom *The Fresh Prince of Bel-Air*, playing the athletic and spirited college student Jackie Ames, the former girlfriend of the show's "Fresh Prince," Will Smith. On the show, Will Smith plays a teenage boy who leaves his family behind in Philadelphia to live with wealthy relatives in the exclusive enclave of Bel Air, California, near Beverly Hills.[35]

Tyra rehearsed at home under her mother's tutelage to win the part of a college student. When she went to the audition for the TV show, she dressed in her trade-mark jeans and white T-shirt, looking every inch the college student, and subsequently won the part. She told the producers she loved to watch Will play a guy in the sitcom who was totally out of his league in the ritzy Bel Air community because on many levels, she related to his character. The producers were also impressed with Tyra's towering height. At 5′ 11″, she'd actually be shorter than Will Smith, who is 6′ 2″. Ironically, Will's real-life wife, Jada Pinkett Smith, had auditioned for the show four years earlier but was passed over by the producers because they thought the 5-foot-tall actress was too short for the role.[36]

As well as giving her an opportunity to flex new skills, Tyra discovered that being on television also made her less threatening and more accessible than she had been as a model. "When people know me as a model they back off. They have trouble relating to the image they see in the magazines. But when they recognize me from the television, they relate to me as he chill-out girl. It's like, 'Hey girl, what's up?' "[37]

Tyra played Jackie Ames for seven episodes, loving every minute of it and claiming it was "a real trip working with Will— I remember it was hard to get through a scene without laughing until I cried." Despite the fun she had on set, Tyra also understood the danger of being typecast at such an early stage in her acting career. She knew it was time to leave the show when "everybody started coming up to me on the street and calling me Jackie Ames," she told *People*.[38]

TYRA CATCHES SINGLETON'S EYE AND HEART

Fortunately, with her modeling gigs, Tyra could afford to quit the show and wait for the right role. "My modeling career gives me the chance to make a lot of money and not have to worry about acting to eat and to live. So I act when I want to or when I find something that's fun or interesting for me to do."[39] For Tyra, that meant she had the luxury to pass on a role in the hit 1993 film, *The Firm*, in which she would have played a woman who seduced Tom Cruise on the beach one night in the Cayman Islands. According to Tyra, the role was too one-dimensional and would have typecast her yet again as just a pretty face. "I don't want to take roles that scream, 'I am so pretty!' " she told *People*.[40]

Fortunately, Tyra's acting talents in *The Fresh Prince* had already caught the attention of filmmaker John Singleton, who directed the acclaimed *Boys n the Hood* movie. Having seen Tyra's work on *The Fresh Prince*, he thought she incorporated flavor into "what could easily have been a throw-away role."[41] Singleton had also seen Tyra on the cover of *Essence* magazine in June 1993 and thought she would be perfect for a role in his next film. Unlike the comedic role she had played on *The Fresh Prince*, this role would be in a serious movie about racial tensions, an issue close to Tyra's heart.

The film *Higher Learning*, which Singleton cast Tyra in, would not only signal Tyra's move to the silver screen but would also expose her to a new kind of celebrity she hadn't been looking for. When she and John Singleton began dating, the media followed every move, including the final one when Singleton dumped her and very publicly broke her heart.

NOTES

1. Pam Levin, *Tyra Banks* (Philadelphia: Chelsea House Publishers, 2000), 43.

2. Ibid., 44

3. Quoted by Tom Gliatto, "Tyrasaurus," *People*, April 11, 1994, www.people.com/people/archive/article/0,,20107829,00.html (accessed May 13, 2009).

4. Ibid.

5. Levin, *Tyra Banks*, 44.

6. Tyra Banks, "An Empire Behind the Scenes," *Newsweek*, October 13, 2008, www.newsweek.com/id/162338 (accessed May 13, 2009).

7. Levin, *Tyra Banks*, 50.

8. Lila Chase, *Totally Tyra: An Unauthorized Biography* (New York: Penguin Group, 2006), 17.

9. Quoted by Gliatto, "Tyrasaurus."

10. Chase, *Totally Tyra*, 17.

11. Levin, *Tyra Banks*, 47.

12. Banks, "An Empire Behind the Scenes."

13. Levin, *Tyra Banks*, 48.

14. Quoted by Gliatto, "Tyrasaurus."

15. "50 Most Beautiful People in the World," *People*, May 9, 1994, www.people.com/people/archive/article/0,,20108020,00.html.

16. Quoted by Chase, *Totally Tyra*, 19.

17. Quoted by Roy H. Campbell, "Breaking Down Barriers," *San Jose Mercury News*, April 14, 2007.

18. Ibid.

19. "How to Date a Supermodel."

20. Levin, *Tyra Banks*, 66.

21. Quoted by Gliatto, "Tyrasaurus."

22. Gliatto, "Tyrasaurus."

23. Chase, *Totally Tyra*, 17.

24. Quoted by Lynn Hirschberg, "Banksable," *New York Times Magazine*, June 1, 2008, www.nytimes.com/2008/06/01/magazine/01tyra-t.html.

25. Ibid.

26. Chase, *Totally Tyra*, 30.

27. Tyra Banks, *Tyra's Beauty Inside & Out* (New York: Harper Collins, 1998), 84–85.

28. Quoted by Hirschberg, "Banksable."

29. Chase, *Totally Tyra*, 30.

30. Quoted by Gliatto, "Tyrasaurus."

31. Quoted by Hirschberg, "Banksable."

32. Levin, *Tyra Banks*, 67.

33. Chase, *Totally Tyra*, 38.

34. Levin, *Tyra Banks*, 67.

35. Chase, *Totally Tyra*, 39.

36. Ibid.

37. Levin, *Tyra Banks*, 67.

38. Gliatto, "Tyrasaurus."

39. Chase, *Totally Tyra*, 40–41.

40. Chase, *Totally Tyra*, 39.

41. Chase, *Totally Tyra*, 40.

Chapter 3

LIGHTS! CAMERA! ACTION!

Tyra's search for just the right film to debut in finally paid off, although not before she fell in love with the man who was producing it! His name was John Singleton, who had become the host of Hollywood by writing and directing the film, *Boys n the Hood*, around the same time Tyra was embarking on her modeling career in 1989.

The coming-of-age movie explored the extreme importance of Black fathers in the lives of their sons, and a boy resisting the temptations of drugs and crime in South Los Angeles. The movie grossed more than $100 million worldwide and inspired blacks all over the world—Tyra included. The movie won two Oscar nominations—for best director and best screenplay. At 23, Singleton became the first African American and the youngest director ever nominated for an Oscar in the best directing category.[1]

Like Tyra's parents, John's had also separated when he was young. Also like Tyra, he had a big dream. Ever since he was nine years old and saw the movie *Star Wars*, John had wanted to become a filmmaker. In March 1993, mutual friends introduced John to Tyra, and he decided to cast her in his third film, *Higher Learning*, based on Singleton's personal experiences while attending college at UCLA in Los Angeles.

ISN'T IT ROMANTIC?

"When I saw her on the runway, it was 'wow, she is so beautiful,' " Singleton told *Ebony*. "What can I say? [Tyra] is a good girl and she is very smart. She has a lot going for her. I want a woman who's got a mind. Tyra helps me out a lot. She helps me unwind [and eliminate] the stress. It's a real crazy business and it's really good to have somebody who understands how difficult it is."[2]

Although they were dating, Tyra still had to audition for the role of Deja, a smart and beautiful track star at the mythical Christopher Columbus University who plays opposite Omar Epps. Featuring Ice Cube, Jennifer Connelly, and Laurence Fishburne, the movie explored stereotyping and racial tensions among first semester freshmen students. Tyra was excited that the movie gave her a chance to express her deep-felt belief to "use what you have to get what you want," a line in the film where she urges her boyfriend to keep trying.[3]

When the press accused Singleton of giving Tyra the part because of favoritism rather than talent, he set them straight. "Tyra is good," he told *People*.[4] "John said, 'Read for it,' " Tyra told *Ebony*, " 'but if you're bad, you don't get it. I'd look like I'm thinkin' with my you-know-what.' " Tyra went on to tell *Ebony* that she took the part of Deja for two reasons: "It's not glamorous, and I liked it that John made her smarter than the guy."[5]

Not that John didn't have any concerns about casting Tyra in the role. Because of his fondness for Banks, he admitted to *Ebony* that it was difficult for him to watch Tyra doing the love scenes with the dashing actor Omar Epps. "It was hard but we got through it," Singleton said. "Nobody knows her like I do."[6]

Their courtship was a slow, leisurely one. Although Tyra was very attracted to John, she wanted to take things slow because she was only 19. When John said he wanted the relationship to be exclusive, she said she didn't want to rush things. However, she relented a bit later when she realized he was really the guy for her. "In front of the Empire State Building, I told him I wanted to be his girl," Tyra confessed in an interview the couple had with *People* magazine about two years later.[7]

BEYOND THE CATWALK

Tyra found her acting gig to be a refreshing and relaxing change form the catwalks. "Modeling is a catfight," she told *Ebony* in 1995, adding that she found the cast of *Higher Learning* peaceable, if sometimes a little dense when it came to history. "John was wearing a pendant [with a picture], and Kristy Swanson [another actor in the movie] goes, 'Who's that? You? Sammy Davis Jr.?' He said, 'No, that's Malcolm X.' She'd never heard of Malcolm X! So John made her read *The Autobiography*."[8]

Tyra had to train for her role by working out with Jeanette Bodin, the head women's track coach at UCLA. She described her training regimen of working out four hours a day, seven days a week as "the biggest athletic challenge to date." But Tyra also felt lucky that her first movie was being directed by someone who truly loved and cared about her.[9]

Tyra also loved John's sense of romance and generosity. During their relationship, he lavished gifts on her and threw her a surprise 20th birthday party on a chartered yacht. But problems arose with the differences in their age and socioeconomic background. John was 24 to Tyra's 19, a big gap at that age. And even though they had grown up just 12 miles apart in Los Angeles, Tyra enjoyed a sheltered life of private school education, while John grew up in a rough neighborhood. As John told *People*, "She never waited no tables. I worked my ass off my whole life."[10] After two years, the couple decided to part, for reasons they chose to keep private. They never lived together because Tyra was too old-fashioned, and John felt they were too young to consider marriage. Both also had hectic and demanding schedules that kept them apart for months at a time.[11]

FLESHING OUT HER CREDITS

After appearing in *Higher Learning*, Tyra was anxious to expand her film credits. What she wasn't willing to do was to take on a role that presented her as a beautiful but dumb bimbo. "I want a meaty role, like an addict or femme fatale. I'd love to be the villain," she told *People*.[12] Tyra also looked up to comics like Jim Carrey, claiming she was most interested in film roles that would let her tap into her sense of humor. Although she didn't know it then, her sense of humor would one day contribute to the overwhelming success of her two reality TV shows, *America's Next Top Model* and *The Tyra Banks Show*.

Meanwhile, to flesh out her itinerary until the right movie came along, and also to continue her goal of giving back, Tyra began accepting offers to lecture to young adults. In 1995, she addressed students at the University of Texas on the topic of "race, beauty, and body image in the modeling industry," explaining that the short, competitive careers of most young models led them to become very insecure. "I do feel the obligation to tell young girls who write to me that 99 percent of the modeling industry is fantasy," she said.[13]

AN OVERNIGHT CHANGE

Ironically, Tyra's next break brought her right back to modeling. Tyra made history with a triple achievement in 1996. She was the first African American woman to pose on the covers of the *Sports Illustrated* Swimsuit Issue, *GQ* (February 1996), and the Victoria's Secret catalogue (1996). In the fall of 1995, *Sports Illustrated* had chosen her along with model Valeria Mazza, a model from Argentina, to grace the cover of the upcoming *Sports Illustrated* Swimsuit Issue, a magazine that has yielded powerful influences on the careers of young models and propelled them into the high-paid ranks of superstardom. Cheryl Tiegs appeared in 10 issues, and Christine Brinkley made the covers for three consecutive years.[14]

The theme of the issue was "South African Adventure" and showed Tyra and Valeria visiting the country for photo shoots. Tyra was photographed on a sunny beach in a skimpy cheetah-skin-print swimsuit. Tyra said the shoot was a defining moment in her life; the day the magazine came out, she got on a plane, and everybody on the plane knew who she was.[15]

COVER GIRL CHALLENGES

Being a cover girl might sound glamorous, but Tyra soon discovered it was no walk in the park. To prepare for the shoot, Tyra had to get up at 3 a.m. in the morning for makeup and hair sessions. The shoot lasted eight hours, or until about 4 p.m., when everyone on the crew took a break. Shooting then resumed until sunset. Tyra said the work was grueling, but that you had to go with the flow if you wanted to stay on the shoot.[16] Tyra later recalled that the *Sports Illustrated* shoots were challenging for another reason. "They were always after me to put on some weight or take off some weight," she told James Brady of *Parade*.[17]

The following year, not to be outdone by *Sports Illustrated*, GQ crowned Tyra "Woman of the Year" and put her on their February cover, making. Tyra the first black woman and model to appear on the cover of the magazine by herself, and not with another model. While thrilled with her success and good fortune, Tyra had the maturity to keep her accomplishments in perspective. While it was nice to be part of history and to be breaking barriers, "it would be even nicer one day to have no more firsts, just 50ths and 60ths and 70ths," she said.[18]

TYRA'S COMMERCIAL SUCCESS SNOWBALLS

All of a sudden, like a shooting star, Tyra was everywhere. On the cover of magazines, on runways, in movies, on calendars, in advertisements, on television series and awards shows, in videos, at celebrity bashes, waving to fans, and flashing her characteristic endearing and alluring smile. Despite her fame, name recognition, plenty of money, and her choice of good-looking male escorts, Tyra had earned a reputation in the fashion industry as someone who was down-to-earth and easy to work with, rather than a typical spoiled brat who was caught up in her fame and fortune. When asked about her success as a model, Tyra told *Ebony*, "Believe it or not, I just really know how to pose well. It took me five years to learn what my best angles are."[19]

After Tyra appeared in *Sports Illustrated* and GQ, she was flooded with offers for big-name commercial work, including two advertising spots aired during the 1995 Super Bowl game, which costs millions of dollars per minute. One such ad, a 30-second commercial for Pepsi, featured Tyra and two other supermodels—Cindy Crawford and Bridget Hall—cooing over a newborn baby. A Nike ad, which ran for a minute, featured Tyra and a wooden puppet called L'il Penny, who hosts a party for her idol Tyra and other celebrities such as Stevie

Wonder. According to Tyra, the ad's catchy refrain caught on. Wherever she went, fans would recognize her as the girl in the ad and would call out, "Stop the car, that's Tyra Banks, fool!"[20]

Not to be outdone by GQ, in 1997, *Sports Illustrated* featured Tyra on the cover by herself, wearing a tiny pink and red polka dotted bikini. Shot in the Bahamas after a previous shoot in Turkey didn't work out, it went on to be one of the magazine's most dynamic covers. Emblazoned across the cover was the issue's first feature for the year— "Nothing But Bikinis." Inside, the magazine devoted 16 pages of photos and text to Tyra.[21]

VICTORIA'S ANGELS GO EVERYWHERE

In 1997, Tyra also became the first African American model to appear in Victoria's Secret catalogue. Uncharacteristically top-heavy for a high-fashion model, Tyra found the pages of Victoria's Secret a natural home, although many people assumed she'd had surgery. (She recently used her new talk show as a forum to prove them wrong, asking the men in the audience to leave while an ultrasound was conducted on her chest.)[22] Gracing the cover in a leopard-print Nicole Miller swimsuit, the catalogue was so well received that the company chose Tyra and fellow model Heidi Klum, Rebecca Romijn, Adriana Lim, and Ines Rivero to be their angels and promote the line of sheer bras and panties while wearing 8-foot-wide wings. The models posed under the tagline, "Good angels go to heaven. Victoria's angels go everywhere."[23]

When Tyra posed for the *Sports Illustrated 1998 Swimsuit Calendar*, it was such an instant best seller that they immediately flew her to Hawaii to shoot the 1999 calendar. Between 1997 and 1999, Tyra also accepted offers to appear in music videos. She starred in singer Lionel Richie's *Don't Want to Lose* as a rising star who rushes in and out of limos, surrounded by bodyguards, to avoid the paparazzi, as well as in the late Michael Jackson's *Black and White* video, George Michael's *Too Funky* video, and Tina Turner's *Love Thing* video.[24]

In 1998, Tyra was featured in the groundbreaking new book, *Skin Deep: Inside the World of Black Fashion Models*. Former Ford supermodel Barbara Summers penned what goes on behind the scenes in the glamorous, controversial, and unique world of black models, including Naomi Campbell. The book recalls a time, however, when African American models were seldom seen on magazine covers, runways, or in advertisements.[25]

In 1999, Victoria's Secret launched a live, 15-minute webcast of 20 models donning their lingerie on a runway in downtown Manhattan. The world's fist cyber fashion show, it almost crashed the Internet when 1.5 million people logged on and eclipsed all events that had ever been broadcast exclusively on the Internet. "Never mind that the images were fuzzy and jumpy. An estimated 1.5 million to 2 million surfers clicked on to the live webcast of the Victoria's Secret annual fashion show last week, eager to watch supermodels Tyra Banks, Heidi Klum and Stephanie Seymour strut their teeny bikinis," reported *Newsweek*, adding that "Heavy traffic (with heavy breathing) on the company's Web site caused major delays, but it wasn't the first time virtual voyeurs have breached the limits of real-time Webcasts. Americans swarmed to their computer screens during the Pathfinder mission to Mars, a live birth by a woman in Florida and the transfer of Keiko the whale to a sea pen in Iceland." According to *Newsweek*, nothing compared to the explosion of hits around the globe—34 million in one day—when the fashion show aired. "In the world of online ogling, one truth is already self-evident: from Monica to Victoria, the thong's the thing," wrote *USA Today*.[26]

The fury continued over Victoria's angels. In 2001, The Victoria's Secret Fashion Show aired a special show on November 15 on ABC that was billed as "the sexiest night on television." Taped live in a tent in New York City's Byrant Park, the "angels" flew over the crowd to the sounds of a live gospel choir. The show pulled in 12 million viewers and cemented Tyra's role as an "angel."

THE $10 MILLION BRA

Tyra then undertook a somewhat different mission for Victoria's Secret, agreeing to a shoot that unveiled the company's $3 million bra, which had been created by jeweler Harrin Winston. Photographers and video crews descended on New York's Fifth Avenue to see Tyra model the most expensive bra on earth. To protect Tyra and her

3-million-dollar bra, she was escorted to the press conference in an armored car. Posing for the press, she removed her clothing to show off the bra as the crowd gasped, then stuck around for the question-and-answer period. When one journalist asked Tyra if she would get to keep the diamond-studded bra, Tyra just replied, "I wish."[27]

In 2004, Tyra modeled an even more expensive bra for Victoria's Secret, a $10 million, 112-carat Mouawad-designed Heavenly '70s Fantasy bra. The brassiere's weighty highlight was a flawless 70-carat pear-shaped diamond in the center. The jeweled bra also was adorned with 2,900 diamonds set in 10-karat white gold. It was featured in Victoria's Secret's Christmas catalog, although there's no word if there were any takers.[28]

TYRA GROWS A MILK MUSTACHE

Following the fashion show, Tyra was approached to do TV commercials for several major products. McDonald's asked her to portray a mermaid in an advertisement called "Gone Fishin'" for the fast food chain's fish products, but what really put Tyra on the map was a series of "milk mustache" ads she did for the National Fluid Milk Processor Promotion Board. The promotion also featured other tops supermodels such as Christie Brinkley, Iman, and Kate Moss.[29]

For her first milk mustache ad, Tyra flew the Concorde in from London. At the studio, she was hustled in for the standard two to three hours of hair and makeup, although according to some, she didn't really need it. "All that stuff about how supermodels don't look beautiful until they've been magically transformed by professionals with mascara and lip gloss is bunk," says Jay Schulberg, author of *The Milk Mustache Book*, a behind-the-scenes look at America's most famous ad campaign, adding that Tyra was as down-home as people said she was. "Tyra wasn't impressed by the studio-catered food spread and asked for a burger and fries."[30]

He added the shoot didn't go quite as they had planned. Tyra slipped into a string bikini, but after taking one look at her, they all knew the photo wouldn't fly for teenage girls. "There was no way that a photo of her in a teeny-weeny itsy-bitsy yellow-gold string bikini would be accepted in publications like *Seventeen*. It was too sexy," said

Schulberg. "So it sat in a drawer until it was pulled out for a one-time-only insertion in *Sports Illustrated's* acclaimed swimsuit issue."[31]

Meanwhile, the photographer—world-famous Annie Leibowitz, wisely suggested they shoot Tyra in something homier and photographed Tyra in her favorite "girlfriend" uniform—a white T-shirt and blue jeans. In the ad, Tyra looks out at her audience of teenage girls and says, "Girls, here's your beauty tip. Think about you and your 10 best friends. Chances are nine of you aren't getting enough calcium. So what? So milk. Three glasses of milk a day give you the calcium your growing bones need. Tomorrow—what to do when you're taller than your date."[32]

The bikini ad finally found a home in the May 1996 *Sports Illustrated* Swimsuit Issue. Tyra looks straight at her mostly male audience and says, "Stop drooling and listen. One in five victims of osteoporosis is male. Don't worry. Calcium can help. So don't sit there gawking at me. Go drink some milk." According to *The Milk Mustache Book,* "Bruce Frisch worked hard to get the copyright. After all, nobody just looks at the pictures in *Sports Illustrated* Swimsuit Issue, do they?"[33]

Tyra also caused lots of commotion when she modeled for an ad for Swatch "skin watches," wearing even less than she had worn in the bikini mustache ad. In fact, for the photo, she modeled nude, wearing just the watch. The ad campaign, "Am I Naked or Am I Not?" commemorated the opening of a swatch store at Macy's Department Store in New York City.[34] Tyra traveled across the United States, Europe, and Asia to model Swatch watches (although she didn't always have to model nude!) and remains a loyal customer to this day. "I must own a Swatch in every color and [by every] designer under the sun."[35]

BIDING TIME BY HELPING OTHERS

Meanwhile, despite her busy modeling career, Tyra never forgot her goal of wanting to use her fame and fortune to help others less fortunate. "The beginning of my modeling career was about myself. It was about how many covers can I get, or how many doors can I knock down— because so many people were telling me as a black model I wouldn't be able to accomplish certain things and I wouldn't be

successful in the fashion industry—so it was all about me, me, me, me!"
she told the *Los Angeles Times*.[36]

True to her word, in 1992, Tyra created a scholarship for African
American girls at Immaculate Heart High School, her alma mater.
Each year, she pays the tuition for one financially disabled student.
Tyra said she had been "very privileged that her mother and
father had sent me to private school" and she wanted other African
American girls who couldn't afford it to experience the same kind of
education.[37]

Tyra also became a spokeswoman for the Center for Children &
Families, a nonprofit organization providing safe houses, food, literacy,
and drug treatment for disadvantaged children and their families in
New York City. "Whenever I'm feeling down and out, the one thing
that I know will make me feel good about myself is helping someone
else," Tyra says in her book, *Tyra's Beauty Inside & Out*. "Many celebrities just lend their name to a pet project, but I like one-on-one contact. Just seeing a child's face brightens my whole day. They're like
my surrogate children. We read together and paint together and every
Valentine's Day they'd give me a huge stack of cards—I've wallpapered
one wall in my house with them."[38]

Tyra said she spent so much time with the kids "that they are not
the least impressed by my celebrity. There is no shame in their game.
They are so comfortable with me they even let me know when they
think I have on too much makeup on TV."[39]

In addition, Tyra sponsored a Kidshare toy drive during Christmas
1997 that she said was "as much fun for me as it was for the kids." Tyra
wanted the kids from the center, who had the desire but not the financial ability, to give someone a gift, to experience the spirit of giving. So
she asked corporations and the general public to donate toys, "and
then we had each child give a gift to another child. I wish I could
describe how seeing all those happy, excited faces made me feel, but I
don't think my words would do it justice."[40]

In 1997, Tyra was honored by the Starlight Children's Foundation
of California for her efforts to help children. While thrilled to receive
their Friendship Award, Tyra said the real prize "is what the kids do
for my heart. It is really true when people say when we volunteer our
time and talents to help others, we're the ones who truly benefit."[41]

NOTES

1. Quoted by Lynn More Norment, "Tyra Banks, On Top of the World," *Ebony*, May 1, 1997, www.highbeam.com/doc/1G1-19383832.html (accessed May 12, 2009).

2. Ibid.

3. Quoted by Pam Levin, *Tyra Banks* (Philadelphia: Chelsea House Publishers, 2000), 69.

4. Quoted by Lila Chase, *Totally Tyra: An Unauthorized Biography* (New York: Penguin Group, 2006), 44.

5. Quoted by Aldore Collier, "John Singleton, Higher Learning in Hollywood," *Ebony*, April 1995.

6. Ibid.

7. Quoted by Chase, *Totally Tyra*, 42.

8. Quoted by Collier, "John Singleton, Higher Learning in Hollywood."

9. Quoted by Chase, *Totally Tyra*, 44.

10. Quoted by Tom Gliatto, "Tyrasaurus," *People*, April 11, 1994, www.people.com/people/archive/article/0,,20107829,00.html (accessed May 13, 2009).

11. Quoted by Collier, "John Singleton, Higher Learning in Hollywood."

12. Quoted by Gliatto, "Tyrasaurus."

13. Quoted by Levin, *Tyra Banks*, 71.

14. Janet Mock, "Tyra Banks Biography," *People* Celebrity Central, www.people.com/people/tyra_banks/biography (accessed May 4, 2009).

15. Quoted by Levin, *Tyra Banks*, 74.

16. Ibid.

17. Quoted by James Brady, "Brady's Bits: Tyra Banks (Supermodel and Actress)," *Parade*, September 25, 2005, www.parade.com/articles/editions/2005/edition_09-25-2005/in_step_with_0 (accessed May 2, 2009).

18. Quoted by Levin, *Tyra Banks*, 76.

19. Quoted by Norment, "Tyra Banks, On Top of the World."

20. Quoted by Levin, *Tyra Banks*, 76.

21. *Sports Illustrated* Swimsuit Issue, Fall 1997, www.sports illustrated.com (accessed May 20, 2009).

22. Paige Wiser, "Can These Starlets Pass Our Breast Test?" *Chicago Sun-Times*, December 4, 2005.

23. "It's No Secret: A Bust-See Web Site," *Newsweek*, February 15, 1999, www.newsweek.com/id/87295/page/2 (accessed May 5, 2009).

24. Quoted by Maria Elena Fernandez, "Tyra Banks Building an Empire," *Los Angeles Times*, December 5, 2005, www.highbeam.com/doc/1G1-140063194.html (accessed May 1, 2009).

25. Barbara Summers, *Skin Deep: Inside the World of Black Fashion Models* (New York: Amistad Press, 1998), 34.

26. Karen Thomas, "Tyra Banks in 112 Carats is Uplifting," *USA Today*, October 11, 2004, www.usatoday.com (accessed May 19, 2009).

27. Ibid.

28. Ibid.

29. Levin, *Tyra Banks*, 77.

30. Jay Schulberg, *The Milk Mustache Book* (New York: Ballantine Books, 1998), 6.

31. Ibid.

32. Quoted by Schulberg, *The Milk Mustache Book*, 54.

33. Ibid., 130.

34. "Supermodel Tyra Banks Introduces Swatch at the New Macy's Union," *Oakland Post*, December 13, 1998.

35. Quoted by Fernandez, "Tyra Banks Building an Empire," *Los Angeles Times*, December 5, 2005.

36. Ibid.

37. Banks, *Tyra's Beauty Inside & Out*, 48.

38. Ibid.
39. Ibid., 184.
40. Ibid.
41. Ibid., 185.

Chapter 4

SUPERMODEL TURNED TEEN ROLE MODEL

As a young woman Tyra was becoming very instrumental in creating a black presence for the mainstream fashion and advertising world. But on a personal level, despite her growing fame and fortune, Tyra remained the same down-to-earth woman she had always been, describing herself as a "stay-at-home" girl—although her home changed in 1995, when she moved from her apartment in New York back to California, where she purchased a half-million-dollar Mediterranean house with a Spanish patio, five bedrooms, and just as many fireplaces in the Hollywood Hills overlooking the San Fernando Valley.[1]

Although the house was a peaceful retreat from her hectic travel schedule, Tyra later said that buying the house may have been a mistake because she often felt so lonely there. She eventually gave the house to her mother and moved again, this time to Orlando, Florida. In Florida, Tyra must have been feeling a lot less lonely, because her Florida pad certainly wasn't what you'd call tiny.[2]

Despite the many changes in her life since she had become a supermodel, a lot of things about Tyra remained the same, and in fact, pretty boring. She still wore her favorite T-shirt and jeans uniform when she wasn't working, and only donned designer clothes when she had to. She remained an avowed teetotaler, with virgin pina coladas her "drink" of choice. Her favorite pastimes weren't going out to expensive restaurants, glamorous night spots, or vacationing in lavish resorts, but hanging around the house watching television and talking on the telephone—something she did quite a bit of when she was strutting the runways of Europe.[3]

A NEW PRESENCE FOR BLACK MODELS

By 1997, Tyra had also created a presence for black models. Although there were other black models working in the early 1980s, including Iman, the exquisite beauty from South Africa who is widely regarded as the first black supermodel, Tyra was one of the first American black models to create a presence for black women in mainstream magazines and television shows. "When I was young, I used to see all these models and actresses appearing on the pages of fashion magazines, but none of them were my skin tone. I am proud to know that a young lady can leaf through the pages of a magazine and see me in an advertisement, in a photo layout, or in an interview," she told *Ebony*.[4]

VOLUNTEERISM AWARDS

Meanwhile, Tyra was also spending a lot of her free time working with charitable organizations. On March 31, 1998, in Washington, DC, Tyra was honored as a featured speaker at the Volunteerism Awards luncheon, an event sponsored by *Seventeen* magazine and CoverGirl cosmetics. Responding to former President Clinton's call for volunteerism and public service, the magazine and cosmetics company partnered together to honor young women who had done extraordinary things for ordinary people. Tyra shared the spotlight with Senator John Warner and young award winners and told the audience, "It's important to love what you see in the mirror, but it's even more important how you feel about what you see in the mirror."[5]

Speaking on behalf of the sponsors, Tyra helped award more than $100,000 in scholarships and U.S. savings bonds to young women between the ages of 14 and 21 who had committed themselves to volunteer service. Winners included 13-year-old Amity Weiss of Ithaca, New York, who organized a children's march and fundraisers for a troubled town in Bosnia, which eventually became Ithaca's twin city, and

Amber Coffman, 13, of Glen Burnie, Maryland, who founded Happy Helpers for the Homeless, which provided food and other necessary items for homeless people living in her hometown and in Baltimore.[6]

After speaking at the awards luncheon, Tyra was surrounded by teenagers who shyly asked her for her autograph. Tyra personally understood what it meant to help others. As she signed, she told the young women, "I'm not usually impressed easily, but I have to say I'm super impressed today!"[7]

If the world had caught up with Tyra, Tyra hadn't quite caught up with the world—or her growing fame, claiming she was always "amazed" when a huge crowd of fans showed up for her autograph, or when photographers "jump in my face," both at her public appearances and in her private life. "Sometimes I turn around to see who they are waiting for, and when I realize that it's me, I have to laugh and shake my head!" she says in her book, *Tyra's Beauty Inside & Out.*[8]

Tyra also continued working to encourage young women to help others less fortunate. That July, she wrapped holiday gifts with volunteers at St. Vincent's Hospital in lower Manhattan with The Children's Hope Foundation, to be given to youngsters with HIV and AIDS that December to kick off the second annual Seventeen/Cover-Girl Cosmetics Volunteerism Awards.[9]

TYRA THE SEX OBJECT

Although Tyra certainly didn't slink around Los Angeles or Orlando in some of the revealing bare-all outfits you see celebrities wearing today—she was usually in her jeans and tees—she was aware that models often became sex objects and was happy to fill the role—in her own way, of course. In a news conference following the 1998 Volunteerism Awards ceremony, *Details* magazine asked how she felt about appearing as a sex symbol. "I'm happy to be a sex symbol. In the modeling industry, there have been very few black commercial sex symbols, so I'm glad to break ground."[10] But Tyra was actually more concerned about changing the image of black women in the media, whom she believed were too often shown in a negative way as overly seductive. "Black women have always been these animalistic erotic creatures. Why can't we just be the sexy American girl next door?"[11]

TYRA INSIDE AND OUT

Tyra was so inspired by the feedback she got from her speeches, and from the avalanche of fan mail she received from young girls who asked her questions about makeup, clothing, boys, exercise, and modeling, that she decided to write a self-help book to share what she had learned from modeling and to serve as a "big sister" to her readers by offering them encouragement and advice on how to get what they wanted from life. With the help of Vanessa Thomas Bush, a magazine editor for *Life*, Tyra scoured her old journals and photo albums and enlisted the help of experts, writing a book covering fashion, fitness, health, beauty, makeup, dating, sex, drugs and alcohol, and other topics. Tyra's book was published in spring 1998. By the end of the year, it had been named one of School Library Journal's "Best Books of 1998."[12]

Tyra said even though there were already "a million books out there that tell you how to apply lipstick," she wanted to "lay it all out on what really makes a woman beautiful," covering everything from sex and dating to substance abuse to self-empowerment. Tyra also wanted to share the beauty and fitness tips she'd picked up and perfected over the past six years by working with some of the finest experts on the planet. As she sat on the floor shuffling through old photos for the book, Tyra said, "I couldn't help but ask myself, 'How did I, Tyra Banks from Inglewood, become a supermodel?' It wasn't that long ago that I was a young girl dealing with the same insecurities, fears, and negative thinking that I read about in the girls' letters every day." In her book, Tyra admits that she is still dealing with a lot of those same issues.[13]

Throughout the book, Tyra inserted personal essays on topics ranging from getting a friend to open up about emotional abuse to her personal memories of disastrous dates. To show young women reading the book that she wasn't born a bombshell—and that she isn't one today unless she's wearing makeup—she scattered pictures of herself at all ages throughout the book, including several untouched photos—complete with puffy eyes, dark circles, zits, and even a mustache shadow.[14]

Tyra wrote that she was aware that many people thought she was "perfect, with not a care in the world. But if those people could only see me the night before a big shoot when I'm locked in the bathroom with a terrible case of stomach cramps, or when I'm holed up in my room feeling down in the dumps and heartbroken over some big breakup."[15]

THE PRICE OF FAME

Tyra also used her book to talk about what it's really like to be famous. "I'm not above the normal human experiences of pain, self-doubt, rejection, and physical imperfections," she wrote. "I know I am successful at my job, yet I do not see myself as this 'famous celebrity' the way others do." Tyra told her readers about the downside of fame, including the "dramatic change" in the way old friends treated and reacted to her, and being surrounded by sycophants who treat her like some kind of royalty or goddess instead of a human being. "I've tried not to let all of this special treatment affect my perspective. It's hard for some people to accept that I can be as good-natured and down-to-earth as I seem. Some think it is all an act."[16]

Case in point was the day Tyra was giving a lecture at Georgetown University, and a testy young woman in the audience challenged her on her subject, which was self-esteem. With a lot of attitude, she asked Tyra, "Why did you come here to speak to us about self-esteem when you have every reason to feel good about yourself? Not every woman can look like you do." Tyra told the woman that "all I can do is try to tell my story openly and honestly of what I have experienced." In her book, Tyra admits that some people resent her "no matter what I say or do." While Tyra says she found the woman's attitude difficult to deal with at the time, "I now realize that I can only be myself and not let the negative energy of others get to me."[17]

TYRA UNTOUCHED

While it's become more common today for celebrities and models to be honest about the miracles of modern-day photography, with its ability to erase wrinkles and pounds and even reshape a model's thighs, Tyra was one of the first to come out of the closet about the transformation that occurred at the hands of makeup artists.[18]

As Tyra's career evolved, she continued to show herself as a "natural woman," appearing on her talk show and in magazines without makeup on so her fans could see her as she really was. And while the book was designed to help other women find their own true inner and outer beauty, as charitable actions often do, it also propelled Tyra to a whole new level. Tyra said writing the book was a turning point in her career, showing the world that being pretty wasn't all that she was about. Tyra said she believed her life's mission was to help others. Although Tyra worked hard to get where she is today, she has never forgotten the people who helped her get there. Tyra dedicated her book to "the women before me who paved the way, to Daddy who paid the way, and Ma who paced the way."[19]

TYRA'S TZONE

Tyra was so thrilled with the success of her book that she started looking around for other ways to help young girls struggling with low self-esteem and a lack of self-confidence. As one of the highest-paid supermodels in the world, Tyra already had the financial resources to help others. She also realized she had a unique talent among famous women for not causing others to feel intimidated by her. And while she wrote her book to answer the many questions she received from young girls, after it was published, she got even more letters than before, making her realize there was still a big need to fill. In 2000, Tyra and her mother Carolyn decided to found TZone through the Tyra Banks Foundation, a leadership program for disadvantaged teenage girls from four high schools in the Los Angeles area.[20]

Free of charge, TZone was designed to enhance independence and self-esteem among teenage girls by offering them a special, one-week overnight summer camping experience with Tyra as their counselor and soul mate! By working with Tyra, the girls would enjoy an open forum for self-expression, get help visualizing personal goals, develop leadership skills, and get motivate to excel academically.[21]

"TZone is really important for girls between the ages of 13 and 15 because it's a time when there's temptation and peer pressure," Tyra told the media. "So many girls feel like they're alone, then they come here and realize they can excel."[22]

The next summer, Tyra and Carolyn opened their fist TZone camp at Big Bear Mountain, a ski resort town located about an hour east of Los Angeles in the San Bernardino Mountain. "I have great memories of camp—just having the camaraderie of girls that weren't from the same background thrown together. That's what happens at my camp."[23] Tyra told PR Newswire that modeling was specifically not open to discussion at TZone. "I want the girls to focus on building their self esteem and image," she said.[24] Tyra was reportedly the happiest camper of them all, hosting late-night singing around the campfire, big-sister mentorship sessions, and lots of other fun activities. "I'm like a big sister to them. I'm a friend and a mentor,"[25] said Tyra, adding she had even become a trained crisis counselor for the camp. "We do a lot of sharing and crying, and the girls are allowed to have a private session with me if they want. I told everyone when we started this thing that I was not going to just put my name on something and not be involved. This is important to me. I am there for the girls. I choose everything. I even choose each and every menu. It's important to me that everything be perfect for the girls."[26]

If the girls began camp by feeling a little intimated by Tyra, they quickly got over it as the week wore on, especially when they were participating in team-building experiences such as ropes courses—with Tyra holding the other end of the rope! By the time camp was over, they were calling Tyra by her camp nickname, "BBQ."[27] "Girls are coming up to me every single day, going, 'I thought you were going to come here in an evening gown with a tiara on a golf cart and be waving to us,'" said Tyra. "They didn't know I was going to be here every single day. I stand up there and I cry with them, and it just shows them that there is humility in everybody and that everybody has insecurities. No matter how successful I am, no matter how big I get, I'm still the insecure skinny eleven-year-old. Yes, I was very lucky, but I take responsibility to give back and show we're all going through the same thing."[28]

In October 2002, Tyra and her TZone camp for girls were featured on an episode of "Life Moments," a daily, one-hour reality series featuring relevant and inspirational stories by and about women and the pivotal moments in their lives. The TV show highlighted how a week-long stay at TZone impacted 13 year-old Shamanda Thomas, a southern California high school student who, prior to her affiliation with TZone, was experimenting with drugs and falling behind in school.[29]

TZONE GOES NATIONAL

Tyra began looking for ways to expand the scope of TZone so that it would become a year-round program rather than just a summer camp. In 2006, Tyra announced on her reality TV show, *America's Next Top Model* that TZone would refocus from running summer camps for girls to supporting organizations that serve women and girls ages 13–35. "TZone is at a very important juncture right now," said Tyra.

> We have evolved from a summer camp for girls in southern California to a national grant-making foundation that will not only raise awareness of the needs of women and girls, but also fund worthy programs. With the reorganization of TZONE, our goal is to help as many girls and women as possible. By making grants to grassroots organizations, we will make a greater impact. I intend to use the content of my talk show and *America's Next Top Model* to inspire women of all ages to achieve success and fulfillment in their lives.[30]

In 2008, to honor Tyra for her work with TZone, *Glamour* magazine named her one of its ten "2008 Women of the Year," an award that Tyra shared with Nicole Kidman, Hillary Clinton, and Jane Goodall for "her unprecedented contributions to the worlds of entertainment, business, sports, fashion, science and politics."[31] The magazine also profiled Tyra in its December 2008 issue, calling her "one of television's fiercest female-power icons. Tyra promotes diverse beauty and realistic body images on her shows, and her charity, the TZone Foundation, funds organizations that encourage and support young women," *Glamour* said.[32]

"NO MORE MODEL GROUPIES"

All work and no play would have made Tyra a dull girl, which she certainly wasn't! When Tyra wasn't involved in work or charities, she actually carved out a little free time for men and dating. After dumping John Singleton, Tyra had a brief fling with pop-music icon Seal. At 33, 10 years Tyra's senior, he was the quintessential "older man" in Tyra's life. But despite his fame, fortune, sexiness, and maturity, Tyra dumped him, too, claiming she no longer wanted to date celebrities or what she described as "model groupies." Seal was crushed, but he eventually got over it and married a close pal of Tyra's—fellow supermodel Heidi Klum. Today, all three are close friends, and Tyra calls Seal "the most special man I know."[33]

After leaving Seal, Tyra began to develop some definite ideas about the sort of men she wanted to see. She decided that married or otherwise attached men were off limits to her, and that she wanted to date men who had a good sense of humor and old-fashioned values —the kind of guy who would have no problem opening the door for her and pulling out her chair, but who would also be liberated enough to agree to splitting a check. Unfortunately, it would be a long time before such a man materialized. Meanwhile, Tyra went through a string of boyfriends who left her disappointed, lonely and/ or brokenhearted.[34]

TYRA MOVES TO ORLANDO

In 2000, Tyra purchased another home outside Orlando, Florida, claiming she wanted to be able to relax in the bright Florida sun and be close enough to hop over to Disney World and other theme parks whenever she wanted—one of her favorite ways to have fun. Tyra also used her time in Orlando to chill out with some of her favorite hobbies, including running, dancing, and combining workouts with dance, including dancing to drums and losing herself in the rhythms. She also spent time listening to her favorite music, including Alanis Morrisette, Snoop, Jewel, and The Cranberries, and going to the movies by herself. An avid basketball fan, Tyra attended Los Angeles Lakers' games when she was in town, and also indulged in one of her all-time favorite pas-times: hitting the thrift shops for vintage jeans and clothing.[35]

TYRA BECOMES A STAR PRODUCER

While running TZone, Tyra also carved out time to appear in more films. Following her role in the *Fresh Prince of Bel Air*, Fox television invited her to appear in three episodes of *New York Undercover*. Then Disney found a starring role for her in the TV movie, *Honey Thunder Dunk*, which was presented on the *Wonderful World of Disney*. It was Tyra's first film for television, and one in which she starred not only in the movie but also as its coproducer. In fact, the other producers had created the story line with Tyra in mind. In the romantic comedy, *Honey Thunder Dunk*, Tyra played a basketball player in the Women's National Basketball Association, an organization for which she was also a spokesperson.[36]

In the summer of 1998, Tyra starred in another romantic comedy called *Love Stinks*. In 1999, Tyra played a starring role in the film *The Apartment Complex*, which aired on the cable channel Showtime.[37] In the late 1990s, word spread that Tyra had embarked on a singing career, a rumor fueled by the British *Sky* magazine, which had misinterpreted headlines in U.S. newspapers claiming that Tyra had gotten "a record deal." In fact, Tyra's record deal was with a cosmetics company, not a record company. Tyra refuted the rumors with humor. "I only ever sing in the shower, and then it's usually just a bit of Alanis Morisette, because I like the screaming."[38]

OPRAH CALLING

By 1999, Tyra had become one of the world's most recognizable teenage role models. But she was about to become even more famous. That year, Oprah personally invited Tyra to join her talk show as a monthly youth correspondent, The two-year stint gave Tyra the opportunity to learn about life from one of her childhood idols, and also gave her the TV experience she'd later need to host her own shows.

During the two-year stint, Tyra and Oprah became close friends and soul mates. "Even though she is one of the richest women in the world, she is the 'realest', most down-to-earth person you'd ever want to meet," said Tyra. "Everyone can relate to her, which is a wonderful quality to have."[39] Tyra also learned from Oprah what made her such a popular and influential star. "The biggest thing about Oprah is her authenticity," she said. "She is so true. There is no pretence to her, and the audience knows it."[40] Ironically, the fans of Oprah's show were discovering the same things about Tyra. According to Warner Brothers, when Tyra appeared on the program, Oprah's ratings spiked by 8–10 percent![41]

While rumors swirled that Oprah was honing Tyra to take over for her when Oprah no longer wanted to be on TV, they were quieted when Oprah renewed her contract in 2008.[42] But there was some truth to the rumor—Tyra did in fact dream of having her own talk show, and had actually been approached by another network to do one. As she confessed to *Ebony*, "I want to be successful across the board. I want an empire like Oprah's. I may do it with a little more cleavage, but I plan to get there."[43]

It was years before Tyra was approached to do her own talk show in 2005—and the first person she turned to for advice was Oprah, who told Tyra that it would be "one of the hardest things she'd ever do, and to call if she needed advice." Jay Leno also offered Tyra some words of wisdom. "Be yourself, listen to your instincts, and remember that people love to laugh."[44] Tyra apparently took their words to heart. When her talk show, *The Tyra Banks Show*, debuted in 2005, it soared off the charts and quickly became the top-rated show in its time slot among women between ages 18 and 35.

Whether or not Tyra was ready to become the Oprah of her generation, her generation was ready for her.

NOTES

1. Pam Levin, *Tyra Banks* (Philadelphia: Chelsea House Publishers, 2000), 17.

2. Ibid., 93.

3. Ibid.

4. Quoted by Lynn More Norment, "Tyra Banks, On Top of the World," *Ebony*, May 1, 1997, www.highbeam.com/doc/1G1-19383832.html (accessed May 12, 2009).

5. Levin, *Tyra Banks*, 18.

6. Levin, *Tyra Banks*, 15.

7. Ibid., 20.

8. Tyra Banks, *Tyra's Beauty Inside & Out* (New York: Harper Collins, 1998), 14.

9. Levin, *Tyra Banks*, 20.

10. "Tyra Banks." *Details Magazine*, May, 1997.

11. Ibid.

12. Levin, *Tyra Banks*, 87.

13. Banks, *Tyra's Beauty Inside & Out*, 13.

14. Ibid., 14.

15. Banks, *Tyra's Beauty Inside & Out*, 13.

16. Ibid., 16.

17. Ibid.

18. Ibid., 17.

19. Ibid., 9.

20. Lila Chase, *Totally Tyra: An Unauthorized Biography* (New York: Penguin Group, 2006), 54–55.

21. Banks, *Tyra's Beauty Inside & Out*, 87.

22. Ibid.

23. Ibid.

24. "Super Model Tyra Banks and Her Tzone Camp for Girls to be Featured on 'Life Moments,'" *PR Newswire*, October 30, 2002.

25. Chase, *Totally Tyra*, 54–55.

26. Ibid., 56.

27. Ibid., 57.

28. Ibid., 57.

29. "Super Model Tyra Banks and Her Tzone Camp for Girls to Be Featured on 'Life Moments.'"

30. "TZONE Foundation Celebrates National Philanthropy Day, Announcing Its First-Ever Grants to Support Women's Organizations," *Business Wire*, November 14, 2006, www.allbusiness.com/services/business-services/3935603-1.html.

31. Laurie Sandell, "Women of the Year 2008," *Glamour.com*, November 11, 2008, www.glamour.com/women-of-the-year/2008/tyra-banks.

32. Ibid.

33. Levin, *Tyra Banks*, 91.

34. Ibid., 92.

35. Chase, *Totally Tyra*, 73.

36. Levin, *Tyra Banks*, 88.

37. Ibid., 90.

38. Ibid., 90.

39. Chase, *Totally Tyra*, 61.

40. Ibid.

41. Ibid., 62.

42. "It's Showbuzz: Chat Show Queen Oprah Grooms Super-model," *Sunday Mercury* (Birmingham, England), March 5, 2000, www.highbeam.com/doc/1G1-67694958.html (accessed May 20, 2009).

43. Norment, "Tyra Banks: On Top of the World."

44. James Brady, "Supermodel Turned TV Star Tyra Banks Dives into the Shark-Infested Waters of Daytime Talk Show," *Parade*, September 25, 2005.

Chapter 5

FROM RUNWAY TO REALITY TV

With her supermodeling success, her success at acting, and her top rating on the *Oprah Show* as "Youth Correspondent," Tyra was on a roll. But she was just warming up! A huge fan of reality TV, especially the shows *The Real World* and *American Idol*, Tyra began wondering if there was room for her in the reality TV world.

One morning while she was hanging out in the kitchen sipping her morning tea, she got a brainstorm—a reality show that would combine the best of *American Idol* and *The Real World* into one reality TV show about the cutthroat world of modeling. She also wanted to show the world what it really took to become a top model. As she had once said to the *Washington Post*, "There are so many people coming up to me and asking me how to get into the modeling business. How can I get all these people off my back?"[1]

Tyra says the idea for the show just came to her. "I was in my kitchen in my underwear looking out the window, and just saw the words *America's Next Top Model* in my head," she told *United Press International*. "I wanted to do a show where people were striving for a goal, winning something that you've worked hard for."[2]

A HIT SHOW IS BORN

Positive that she had an idea the public would love, Tyra asked her agent what he thought. Ken Mok, the man who would become Tyra's coproducer, wasn't sold on the idea at first—for a number of reasons he later admitted. But he did admit that reality shows were gaining ground. By 2002, CBS had enjoyed great financial success with *Survivor* and *Big Brother*, and Tyra's idea would combine elements of both. Mok, who had produced *Making the Band*, a reality show that documented the creation of O-Town, a boy band, told the *New York Times*,

> I knew we were entering into a new territory that was about to explode, but I had no interest in fashion, and all I knew about Tyra was her *Sports Illustrated* swimsuit cover and that, at the time, she had dated the basketball star Chris Webber. I'm more of a football guy than a model guy, and I thought, "This is going to be a vanity project where I will do all the work and she will get an executive-producer credit." But five minutes into the conversation, I realized that she was very driven and keenly smart. I'm an incredibly ambitious person, but Tyra makes me look lazy![3]

Tyra and Ken decided to team up as coproducers and take Tyra's concept to the networks. "Everybody was willing to take a meeting with Tyra," Mok recalled to the *New York Times*, "because it's always fun to have a meeting with a supermodel. But they were always surprised by how serious and determined she was." Tyra and Mok eventually sold *America's Next Top Model* to UPN, a fledging network that later combined with WB to become The CW network, which has a target audience of 18- to 34-year-olds who are mainly women.[4]

The new series was a hit despite scant initial promotion. "That spoke volumes to me about this connection she had with women. It was a lot deeper than just being a model," James Paratore, executive vice president of Warner Bros. Domestic Television Distribution and president of Telepictures Productions, which distributes Tyra's talk show and co-owns it with Tyra's firm, Bankable Productions, told *Forbes* magazine. By the time Tyra launched her talk show in 2005, she had established such strong rapport with her viewers that 90 percent of her *Top Model* fans tuned in to watch her talk show."[5]

TYRA GOES BEHIND THE CAMERA

Along with Moy, Tyra ran and continues to run every aspect of *America's Next Top Model*. More than just showing up for work and being on camera, Tyra also hires and fires directors, handles the finances, chooses shoot locations, and spends hours every day editing a slew of material related to the show. As Tyra told Diane Sawyer on *The Early Show*, "I am such a control freak and such a perfectionist, every single frame of that show, every music cue, the lighting, I am so involved with it."[6]

As everyone knows by now, the show follows 13 young women of various backgrounds, shapes and sizes, who live together in a lavish New York penthouse for eight weeks and vie for a modeling contract. The drama exposes the transformation of everyday young women into potentially fierce supermodels, as they face weekly tests that determined who can make the cut. The finalists compete in a highly accelerated modeling boot camp, a crash course to supermodel fame that includes mentoring by Tyra as well as exposure to high-profile fashion industry gurus, all under 24-hour-a-day surveillance of the show's cameras, which chronicle every move.[7]

Assisting Tyra in instructing and chiding the girls to perfection is Jay Manual, a witty and sometimes sarcastic makeup artist and photo director, and J. Alexander, who teaches the girls how to work the runway and judges their performance. In many ways, the show parallels another hit reality show, *Survivor*. At the end of each episode, a panel of judges from the modeling world, including Tyra, rate the girls on their modeling style, physical fitness, publicity skills, and ability to adapt to photo shoots and eliminate the weakest contestant. The winners receive representation with a modeling agency, a contract with a cosmetics company like Revlon or CoverGirl, and a photo spread in a fashion magazine such as *Marie Claire* or *Elle*.[8]

Tyra told the *New York Times Magazine* that the show is about much more than modeling—it's about life. "We're in a day and age when these kids want instant success, and they don't want to work for it. I feel tough love prepares these girls," Tyra said, defending her often sarcastic and cutting style with the contestants. In one episode, she screams at a contestant so loudly her eyes threaten to burst out of her head. But she told the *Times* she also had another motive to being critical. People would rather watch nasty than nice, and "I've got to sell a TV show."[9]

The competition on the show can be so fierce that Tyra doubts she would have made the cut herself. "I always say that if I tried out for *America's Next Top Model* when I first started modeling, I wouldn't have made it," she told *New York Times Magazine*. "Physically, I would have been fine, but personality-wise, I would have felt like I was in front of college admissions people and that I had to say the right answer."[10]

HERE COMES THE JUDGE

As with the models, *America's Next Top Model* also has a revolving door of judges. In the first season, the judges included *Marie Claire* editor Beau Quillian, fashion designer Kimora Lee Simmons, and former supermodel Janice Dickinson. While Kimora remains a close friend of Tyra's (but is no longer on the show), Dickinson was very publicly booted off the show after dissing the models as well as Tyra and the show, too. Tyra said everyone on the show "loved to hate Janice" because she had a very opinionated and strong way of speaking to the girls—"and all of it doesn't get on camera," she said, referring to Janice's habit of criticizing the models for things about themselves they couldn't change, such as having feet that were too big.[11]

Tyra's latest victim was actress and model Paulina Porizkova, who was fired in May 2009 after serving as a judge for a year on the show. While Tyra told the media she axed Porizkova for budgetary reasons, the actress had other ideas.[12] "The reason I was told I was fired was because, it seemed that *America's Next Top Model* has gotten too fat and they needed to cut some fat and the fat was me," she said in an interview on *The Early Show*. "So I figured it was either that or my gigantic huge ego. Which I wasn't aware of until I was told by the producers that I have an ego problem."[13]

A BIG HIT

Despite the internal commotion and politics, after one season on the air, it was clear that *America's Next Top Model* was not a one-hit wonder. The viewers loved the show—and the catfights off stage even more! In 2004, in one of the slowest syndication development seasons on record, the show was only one of two to receive a green light.

"Young women today have no bias toward network TV, so stations need to buy franchises to attract them," Paratore told *The Early Show*. "And that franchise is Banks." According to UPN, the show had delivered the network's highest series ratings ever in its time period among women ages 18–34.[14]

Although Tyra was excited by the ratings, she told UPN that she was even more excited about the opportunity to be a creative force, and claimed that *America's Next Top Model* was the most satisfying work of her career. "It's been really stressful, my stomach aches, and I haven't had a manicure in months, but it's something I've always wanted to do. It's nice to finally be in charge," she said.[15]

Although Tyra is not shy about debating the merits of her aspiring supermodels, she doesn't cast a vote unless the judges are deadlocked. However, she does announce the winner, usually in a stern, maternal tone that makes it sound as if the models' entire lives are dependent upon the results.[16]

THE PRESS WEIGHS IN

Despite the show's incredible ratings, the media was mixed in its reviews. Some claimed the show actually managed to combine life lessons with fashion sense. Others wondered if the show's goal of turning the winner into a top model was actually realistic or doable.

"Like many reality shows, 'Top Model' offers a mix of wish fulfillment and humiliation," reported Lynn Hirschberg in the *New York Times Magazine*.

The girls are cast as much for their ethnic diversity as their pulchritude —they're the prettier, thinner sisters of the 'Tyra Show' audience: urban and a little rough around the edges. But this doesn't mean there is harmony on the show—catfights abound. The girls are often mean to one another, and Banks is both supportive and tough: she consistently tries to redirect their priorities but isn't above shaming them to the point of tears. In recent cycles, the sincerity and gravity of her approach has been mitigated by her increasingly theatrical behavior—Banks has a fondness for breaking into song and shifting into strange, indecipherable accents. For its loyal, almost fanatical audience, the show deftly balances "Pygmalion," soap-opera antics, fashion-world weirdness and life lessons.[17]

On the other hand, according to Hirschberg, the show had also been derided by the fashion industry as unrealistic. Although the winner receives a modeling contract with Elite Model Management, a Cover-Girl campaign, and a layout in *Seventeen*, "no winner on the show has yet to achieve commercial success as a model," she pointed out. But according to Tyra, it was all part of the plan. "Of course I know what a supermodel looks like, but I also know that a show filled with 13 girls that have the right look and no personality is not going to be relatable or watched," she told Hirschberg. "I'm more interested in fighting for the racial mix of the cast. Dark-skinned black girls are usually not famous —if you think of black girls, it's light-skinned girls like me or Beyoncé or Halle Berry. When I'm casting a dark-skinned black girl on 'Top Model,' I'm sending a message to the little girl watching at home that she is beautiful."[18]

HEIDI KLUM CHIMES IN

Tyra got unconditional support from an unexpected source—fellow supermodel Heidi Klum, a friend of Tyra's who just happened to host a very similar rival reality TV show called *Project Runway*.

"I'm not surprised that Tyra has achieved such phenomenal success," she wrote in *Time*.

> She's one of the most hardworking people I know—I've seen her go straight from a late night of press to an early-morning shoot with no complaints. Even more important, she is passionate about her projects and compassionate toward the people involved in them. Her appeal is obvious to anyone who knows her, whether personally or professionally or just from her shows. She is dynamic, positive and real, and we are only at the beginning of her special brand of global domination.

According to Klum, besides being a very savvy business mogul, Tyra was also a wonderful friend.

> Everyone knows Tyra as supermodel, as host and producer of *America's Next Top Model* and her own talk show, and as whip-smart business mogul. She is all those things. But I also know her as a close friend. When I started as an "Angel" for Victoria's Secret, Tyra was already an established pro there. During lunch, I'd grill her about the business:

whom she would recommend as an accountant, an attorney, a business manager. Not everyone was, let's say, superfriendly, but Tyra was always nice. She shared her experience and knowledge with me.[19]

Heidi said that Tyra also never failed to help others achieve their dreams and goals.

In this industry there are a lot of people who don't want to help each other, but I guess Tyra was and is secure because she was always willing to share what she had learned—and, trust me, I asked a lot of questions. That open, warm side of her was more apparent as we became friends and spent a lot of time together at shoots. Tyra and I could always be goofy together and remind each other that, hey, this is fashion, not life or death. On the flip side, when situations got too crazy, we could always turn to each other for a reality check.[20]

TYRA FINALLY GETS A TALK SHOW

With *America's Next Top Model* on cruise control, Tyra began thinking more about her goal to have her own Oprah-like talk show. "That's my Mama," Tyra told *Vanity Fair*, claiming that Oprah had been her mentor and that one reason she also wanted to have a talk show on day time TV was because she felt it would give her an opportunity to help more women. "As the executive producer and host of *America's Next Top Model*, I got a chance to really mentor all the girls in the house and get deeply involved in whatever conflict was going on. That's turned into me wanting to do it on a daily basis," she told *Vanity Fair*.[21]

In fact, the executives at Telepictures had been trying to talk Tyra into doing a daytime talk show for five years, claiming she seemed very comfortable, had a real point of view, and was willing to share her life —one real key to talk-show success. Tyra turned them down when she was 25, claiming she just didn't have enough life experience. But by the time she turned 31, she felt she was ready, having succeeded in a lot of different facets of the business.[22]

In fall 2005, Tyra decided to go for it, taking the advice of mentors Oprah and late-night show host Jay Leno. She told James Brady in an interview with *Parade* that she wasn't sure her show would fly. "I'm very aware of the odds against any new talk show making it on TV. I want to find out my quirks, my strengths and weaknesses. I want to have a show that people haven't seen before," she told him.[23]

"So you're going to be rich?" Brady asked her. "I hope so," Tyra answered. "The money means I can get a house for my brother (an Air Force veteran of 20 years). I bought a house for myself, but it was too big, so I gave it to my mother. In the beginning of my career, it was all about myself—me, me, me. Now it's about helping other girls. It's so important to give back."[24]

Tyra said she also wanted to show people she could do a show that didn't involve modeling, adding that she was prepared to work hard to earn the respect of her coworkers—something she had already had to do with *America's Next Top Model.* "On the set of *America's Next Top Model*, every day was at first a fight because some people thought I was just a model posing as an executive producer," Tyra told *The Early Show.* "People who had positions lower than mine didn't accept me as their boss. After a while, a couple of them apologized for doubting me so much. I had the power to fire those people, but I just wanted to prove them wrong." Tyra said she planned to take that same attitude into syndication, even though she was well aware of the failure rate. "I'm very inspired by the words 'no' and 'can't,'" she said. As well as host, Tyra would be serving as executive producer on *The Tyra Banks Show*, a much bigger challenge than what she had already done for *America's Next Top Model.* UPN buys 13 episodes of *America's Next Top Model* at a time. By way of contrast, Telepictures planned to produce 175 episodes of *The Tyra Banks Show* every year.[25]

TYRA'S TALK SHOW MENTOR

Guiding Tyra as she developed her talk show formula was Lisa Hackner, senior vice president of development for Telepictures Productions, the arm of Warner Bros. Domestic Television Distribution that produced the show. Hackner, like Tyra, was also a success story, and the perfect person to mentor Tyra. She got her start at Telepictures in 1990 as a receptionist and climbed the ranks, priding herself on developing daytime shows, such as *The Rosie O'Donnell Show*, that capitalized on the personality of the host.

For Tyra's talk show, Hackner wanted to show a "real" Tyra that would employ the runway that was emblematic of the model's career. "We're not trying to fit a square peg into a round hole," Hackner said.

> Tyra is an incredible talent and we're building the show around her. There is really not a talk show on the air right now that is geared toward a younger female audience who are beginning that journey in life. Because of Tyra's background and her ability to speak out about a broad range of subject matter and topics, she can speak to these younger women about the things she cares about. She comes to meetings with a notebook full of ideas and with things typed out, ready to present. She doesn't just have an opinion; she comes fully prepared.[26]

Tyra and Hackner bonded quickly. Appearing on *The Early Show*, Tyra said that "Lisa has a great feel for the demo we are going after. She is so passionate, and she is an amazing brainstormer. She has a great spin on how to make people think they are seeing something they've never seen before."[27]

In the show's pilot, Tyra gave viewers a glimpse of what she looked like without all the tricks of the trade, in an attempt to close the gap between reality and Hollywood glamour. "Tyra asked a lot of questions and then listened to what people have to say," Hilary Estey McLoughlin, executive vice president and general manager of Telepictures told *The Early Show*. "She honed in on what people were thinking and got them comfortable enough to tell her." "Tyra is one of those amazing people who is so multi-talented," agreed Dawn Ostroff, UPN's president of entertainment. "She was able to make *Top Model* a compelling television show by recognizing what would make women want to see these young women struggle, and then hopefully achieve their dream and aspirations."[28]

TYRA TALKS UP A STORM

The Tyra Banks Show debuted on September 12, 2005, with guests making their appearance by walking down a runway, Tyra explaining to her audience that her talk show was definitely not a clone of *America's Next Top Model*, but that she wanted to incorporate a runway in her talk show as an important symbolic gesture. "The reason I wanted a runway onstage is that I feel like it's an intimidating thing for most people. I wanted to spin that and make it an empowering place so that women on my stage—once they've accomplished something or expressed themselves—then can get up on that runway and celebrate it. They have so much fun, they don't want to get off."[29]

Tyra kicked off her first show with Grammy-winning artist India Arie performing her latest inspirational anthem, *Just for Today*, the theme song to *The Tyra Banks Show*. Tyra then gave a Cincinnati woman a life changing makeover that would transform her inside and out. Plus, Tyra and her entire audience revealed their true beauty to the TV cameras when they simultaneously removed all their makeup in the biggest make under in talk show history!

"On the talk show the statuesque host truly has come into her own," wrote the *New York Times Magazine*. "She is 25 pounds heftier than the typical model, and she relishes debunking the glamorous illusions of supermodels to reveal herself as a cellulite-prone, baggy-eyed average gal. She gleefully shows unretouched photos of herself (before an editor has trimmed extra inches from her thighs and waist)."[30]

If some scoffed when Banks retired from modeling at 32 and set out to produce and star in her own talk show, it appears she had what it took. In its second season, *The Tyra Banks Show* was the talkfest most watched by women ages 18–39, according to its producers.[31]

The *Miami Times* was one of many publications to rave about the show, claiming Tyra had "launched a movement encouraging women everywhere to embrace their inner-beauty." It stated, "Created as the voice of a new generation, *The Tyra Banks Show* focuses on the dreams, hopes and challenges of today's young women. The goal is to empower women to be the best they can be for themselves, their families and their communities. To this end, Tyra brings the first runway to daytime TV as a place for women to strut and be proud when they need an instant injection of self-confidence."[32]

TYRA'S 34 C'S ARE ALL TYRA

Tyra proved early on that nothing was too sacred to discuss on her talk show, filling her program with topics that had never been addressed on national TV, and even using some shows to debunk rumors about herself that had been circulating since she had become a top supermodel.

In one of her earliest shows, Tyra deflated the rumor that her voluptuousness was the result of plastic surgery by inviting a plastic surgeon on the show to examine her and give her a sonogram. "I'm tired of this rumor. It's something that's followed me forever," the supermodel told her audience. After Tyra asked the men in the audience to leave, Dr. Garth Fisher of ABC's *Extreme Makeover* performed a touch test and then the sonogram. He concluded: "Tyra Banks has natural breasts; there are no implants." Tyra replied, "By no means am I saying a breast implant is a bad thing, but it's not a choice that I made. But it's something that a lot of the public . . . think that I have, and that's so frustrating for me." Tyra, who was still modeling for Victoria's Secret at the time, also displayed how her push-up bra exaggerated her body. Always one for full disclosure, Tyra then added that not *everything* about her was real. "I got fake hair, y'all. I got fake eyelashes." The hour-long show was, as Tyra declared, "all about breasts!" It also featured lessons on proper fitting and an appearance from a slimmed-down Anna Nicole Smith.[33]

On her November 18, 2005, segment, Tyra revealed another part of her anatomy on her episode devoted to pursuing a beautiful booty. Tyra revealed her own "dimpled butt" and received endermologie treatment on the set.[34]

TYRA'S FAT SUIT EPISODE

Tyra was most interested in using her talk show to empower girls and women, which she did by exposing societal myths about beauty and dispensing useful information. One of Tyra's most high-profile episodes was in October 2005 when she decided to wear a fat suit to experience how society abused obese women. Tyra came up with the idea after having breakfast with friends one day. "There was every race at the table, gay and straight but when the subject of obesity came up, my friends started talking in a rude way."[35] To test the prejudice, Tyra climbed into a prosthetic suit that added 200 pounds to her frame and walked around a trendy neighborhood in Los Angeles as a 350-pound woman. "It seemed like the last form of open discrimination that's OK, and I decided to put on a 350-pound suit myself and live that life for a day and see what happens," she told *AP Radio*. "And it was one of the most heartbreaking days of my life. I started walking down the street and within ten seconds, a trio of people looked at me and snickered, and started laughing in my face. And I had no idea it was so blatant."[36]

In another episode, Tyra reiterated her stance to "just say no" to drugs by exploring fellow model Kate Moss's recent cocaine bust, saying she was sad to hear of the scandal because she admired Moss as a fellow supermodel and fashion pioneer. Tyra used the publicized bust to put out a call to the modeling agency bosses to make a more concerted effort to police the modeling business for drugs so that Kate Moss would be its last victim. "It kind of angers me and it saddens me that Kate Moss is becoming this poster child for this, but, at the same time, when something negative happens, something good hopefully comes out of it. So, maybe this is sending a message that this is a problem in the modeling industry and something needs to be done about it," she said on her talk show. "Hopefully, Kate, what you are going through . . . is helping so many young women."[37]

TYRA'S X-RATED EPISODE

On a lighter note, and as further proof that Tyra was able to tap into "girlfriend power" for just about any woman, in one highly-publicized episode, she confronted the porn star, Tyra Banxxx, who had stunned Tyra by appearing on the front cover of porn industry magazine, *Xtreme*, dressed up to look like the real Tyra. Tyra invited Banxxx, whose real name is Alana, on the show to talk things over and to also try to persuade the young woman to drop her stage name and go into a more wholesome line of work. Tyra told Banxxx she had initially done a double take when she saw the cover of *Xtreme*. "For a second I was like, 'Did they put my head on someone else's body?' I thought that it really did look like me. The first thing that went through my head . . . it wasn't anger, it was more of a curiosity, and an empathy like, 'Where does this girl come from . . . and what led her to this?'" As the conversation progressed, Tyra talked Banxxx into retiring her name. Banxxx insisted she had never meant to offend Tyra, who had been her childhood idol and an inspiration to her. "Growing up, everyone always said I should be a model and everyone said I looked like you." To thank Alana for giving up her X-rated name, Tyra offered to help her find more meaningful modeling gigs outside the porn world.[38]

I'M NO OPRAH!

When asked about the raging success of her talk show, Tyra told *Fortune* that she had taken her cue from Oprah, Martha Stewart, and other great women leaders in the United States. "It's not really a talk show. It's a woman's guide to life. It's topical, connected to the news, but we do fashion and fun stuff. It's like different pages or sections in a women's magazine," she said.[39] But Tyra made it clear she wasn't happy about being called "a young Oprah. I lost a lot of sleep about that early on. The next Oprah! Damn, I don't compare! My mother told me to just forget about that," she told *Fortune*. "Oprah has been an incredible success for 20 years, and I'm just starting. The biggest thing about Oprah is her authenticity. She is so true. There is no pretense to her, and the audience knows it."[40]

Tyra told *Fortune* that without Oprah's help she never would have gotten where she was today. "She's been really helpful. She told me life is going to change, and she's right. Oprah and Martha Stewart are the two women I admire the most. They are two brands. Their vision is clear and cohesive. Who can say? Maybe one day I can be like that. You have to keep that level of authenticity and not do anything that would cheapen your image from a product standpoint."[41]

NOTES

1. Quoted by Lila Chase, *Totally Tyra: An Unauthorized Biography* (New York: Penguin Group, 2006), 64.

2. "Model Tyra Banks Wants an 'Oprah' Empire," *United Press International*, March 7, 2004, www.upi.com/Entertainment_News/ 2004/03/07/Model-Tyra-Banks-wants-an-Oprah-empire/UPI- 23251078684852 (accessed June 4, 2009).

3. Lynn Hirschberg, "Banksable," *New York Times Magazine*, June 1, 2008.

4. Ibid.

5. Kiri Blakeley, "Tyra Banks on It," *Forbes* (July 2006), www.forbes.com/free_forbes/2006/0703/120.html (accessed June 4, 2009).

6. Page Albiniak, "Two for the Show: Banks and Hackner Pair Up on New Program," *The Early Show*, May 30, 2005, www.highbeam .com/doc/1G1-133052289.html.

7. Ni'Cole Gispon, "UPN Picks Up a Second Cycle of America's Next Top Model," *PRNewswire*, June 25, 2003, www2. prnewswire.com/cgi-bin/stories.pl?ACCT=104&STORY=/www/story/ 06-25-2003/0001971931&EDATE= (accessed June 2, 2009).

8. Quoted by Chase, *Totally Tyra*, 39.

9. Quoted by Hirschberg, "Banksable."

10. Albiniak, "Two for the Show."

11. Ibid.

12. Ibid.

13. Stephen M. Silverman, "Why Tyra Banks Fired Paulina Porizkova," *People*, May 18, 2009, www.people.com/people/article/ 0,,20279645,00.html (accessed June 4, 2009).

14. Gispon, "UPN Picks Up a Second Cycle of America's Next Top Model."

15. Ibid.

16. Ibid.

17. Quoted by Hirschberg, "Banksable."

18. Ibid.

19. Heidi Klum, *Time*, April 30, 2006, www.time.com/time/ magazine/article/0,9171,1187401,00.html (accessed June 5, 2009).

20. Ibid.

21. Michael Roberts, "America's Next Top Mogul," *Vanity Fair*, February 2007, www.vanityfair.com/fame/features/video/2007/tyra _video200701.

22. Albiniak, "Two for the Show."

23. James Brady, "Brady's Bits," *Parade*, September 25, 2005, www.parade.com (accessed June 6, 2009).

24. Ibid.

25. Albiniak, "Two for the Show."

26. Ibid.

27. Ibid.

28. Ibid.

29. Quoted by Chase, *Totally Tyra*, 73.

30. Hirschberg, "Banksable."

31. Andy Serwer, "From Top Model to Young Oprah," *Fortune*, February 15, 2006, money.cnn.com/magazines/fortune/fortune _archive/2006/02/20/8369125/index.htm (accessed June 6, 2009).

32. "Tyra Banks to Host Her Own Talk Show," *Miami Times*, September 13, 2005, www.highbeam.com/doc/1P1-117231755.html (accessed June 8, 2009).

33. *The Tyra Banks Show*, www.tyrashow.com (accessed June 2, 2009).

34. Ibid.

35. "Tyra Banks Goes Undercover as Obese Woman," *AP Radio Online*, November 2. 2005, www.apradio.com (accessed June 8, 2009).

36. Ibid.

37. "Banks Calls for Drug Policing after Moss Scandal," *WENN News*, November 9, 2005, www.imdb.com/news/wenn/2005-11-09 (accessed June 8, 2009).

38. "Tyra Confronts Porn Doppelganger Banxxx," *WENN News*, October 5, 2006, www.imdb.com/news/wenn/2005-10-05 (accessed June 9, 2006).

39. Serwer, "From Top Model to Young Oprah."

40. Ibid.

41. Ibid.

Model Tyra Banks wears a satin bikini at the Victoria's Secret fashion show on February 3, 1999, in New York. (AP Photo/Mark Lennihan)

U.S. top model Tyra Banks presents an evening gown by Victoria's Secret as part of the Cinema Against AIDS 2000 gala event to benefit the American Foundation for AIDS Research in Cannes, French Riviera, May 18, 2000. (AP Photo/Lionel Cironneau)

Supermodel Tyra Banks holds Bethany Grace Essary, 4, of Oaks, Oklahoma, on October 25, 2000, in New York. Essary is one of five Angels in Action award winners for her courage in surviving third degree burns over much of her body. This was the first year for the award, given by Georgia-Pacific to children who performed heroic and courageous deeds in their community. (AP Photo/Georgia-Pacific, Tina Fineberg)

Model Tyra Banks arrives for the 61st Annual Golden Globe Awards on January 25, 2004, in Beverly Hills, California. (AP Photo/Kevork Djansezian)

Tyra Banks arrives at the Legends Ball, an award ceremony hosted by Oprah Winfrey honoring women who paved the way in arts, entertainment, and civil rights, May 14, 2005, in Santa Barbara, California. (AP Photo/Michael A. Mariant)

Model and talk show host Tyra Banks takes questions from television critics during the presentation of her upcoming talk show The Tyra Banks Show at the 2005 Summer Television Critics Association Press Tour, July 18, 2005, in Beverly Hills, California. (AP Photo/Damian Dovarganes)

Tyra Banks, right, executive producer and host of America's Next Top Model, *and Danielle Evans, the show's 2006 winner, arrive for the announcement of the CW Network premiere fall schedule in New York, May 18, 2006. (AP Photo/ Bebeto Matthews)*

In this photo released by Warner Brothers, talk show host Tyra Banks sits down with Senator Barack Obama (D-ILL) and suggests he gives a crystal ball to his wife, Michelle, to celebrate their 15th wedding anniversary. When Tyra asks what he sees in the crystal ball Obama replies, "I see the White House right there." (AP Photo/Warner Bros, Jason Kempin)

Tyra Banks accepts the Media Award during The BET Honors, *January 12, 2008, in Washington. The show honors the achievements of distinguished African American leaders. (AP Photo/Jacquelyn Martin)*

Tyra Banks accepts the Outstanding Talk Show/Informative Award at the Daytime Emmy Awards on August 30, 2009, in Los Angeles. (AP Photo/Chris Pizzello)

Chapter 6

TYRA'S MEDIA TIRADES

In 2005, Tyra decided to say goodbye to modeling so she could focus on her reality TV shows, *America's Next Top Model* and *The Tyra Banks Show*. Already highly paid—at her peak she could earn $50,000 a day and had a lingerie contract worth $4 million a year—her fortune as the next Oprah Winfrey proved to be even larger, with her talk show in 190 markets and Tyra owning a hefty stake in it. In fact, in 2005, Tyra was now earning upward of $18 million, far more than most supermodels earn, and was ranked number 84 on *Forbes*'s "Celebrity 100 list."[1]

ALL WORK AND NO PLAY

But Tyra was beginning to feel the effects of churning out 13 new weekly episodes of *America's Next Top Model* every six months, along with 170 episodes a year for *The Tyra Banks Show*. From August to December 2005, she worked 12 hours a day, seven days a week, taping two talk show episodes three days a week, daily segments for *Top Model*, and preparing for her last fashion show for Victoria's Secret. She awoke at 4 a.m., was in makeup by 5 a.m. and ran on three or four hours of sleep each night. "There was a burning in my stomach every single day," she told the *New York Times*.[2]

Something had to go, and Tyra already knew it would be modeling, having had a premonition that she would stop modeling before she reached the age of 30. "When I was 18 in Milan, they asked me about my dreams and goals, and I said, 'I'm going to retire from modeling when I'm 23 or 24 and have my own talk show! Okay, I was wrong on the age part."[3]

Tyra prepared a special show to pay tribute to her career as a top model, with highlights from her last catwalk appearance at a Victorian's Secret Fashion Show. She even invited her mother Carolyn to come on the show and quiz her about her career. But Carolyn, unbeknownst to Tyra, decided to turn the show into a real tribute to Tyra by inviting her daughter's family and friends to join her on the show.

As Tyra's father, brother, grandfather, grandmother, and numerous friends walked out onto the studio stage, Tyra was so overwrought with emotion that the producers had to cut to commercials so she could dry her tears and regain her composure. The tears started again when loyal friends and fellow stars like Seal, Ricky Martin, and one-time rival Naomi Campbell came on the show to wish the model the best. "I can't believe that I'm finally doing this, but it's time for me to hang up my wings and me hanging up my wings does signify me hanging up my entire modeling career," she told the audience.[4]

TYRA EXITS THE CATWALK IN A BLACK SATIN CORSET

Tyra's last modeling gig was a Victoria's Secret Fashion Show on December 6, 2005, when the never-shy host went out in style wearing a red lace bra and underwear with a belt made of military medallions. As reporters thronged the runway, Tyra could hardly overcome her joy. "I'm not just retiring from the runway, I'm retiring from modeling. God, I love saying that!" she told *Forbes* magazine, adding, "When I was 18, my mom said I had to have a plan. I decided I'd leave on top. I want to be like athletes who seem stuck in time. When you see them at 50, you can say they can probably still run like a champ."[5]

During the last fashion show, Tyra joked that retiring from modeling finally gave her the power to wear what she wanted to wear during shoots—and she didn't miss the chance to go full tilt on her wardrobe.

Permitted to choose her own wardrobe for the Victoria's Secret shoot for the first time ever, she stunned the audience by strolling down the aisle in a black satin corset and a push-up bra with a beaded organza cape adorned with feathers. "I chose my three favorites. I've never had the clout before. Retiring is Good," she later told *Cosmopolitan* magazine.[6]

The other Victoria's Secret models working the show, including Gisele Bündchen, Naomi Campbell, and Heidi Klum, persuaded Tyra to take her wings home with her, which Tyra thought a befitting gift. "It's really a big deal because you never get to take the wings home because Victoria's Secret loves to display them in museums."[7]

A few years later, in 2008, when Tyra was chosen as one of eight winners of *Cosmopolitan* magazine's "Fun Fearless Phenoms" awards, she reiterated her mother's wise council that she leave modeling before it left her. "My mom encouraged me to look at modeling like being an athlete: You have a limited number of years 'in the game' with attention on you. Then they move on to someone younger and hotter. I knew one day I wouldn't be the 'It Girl' anymore and I'd better plan ahead."[8]

With modeling gigs finally off her plate, Tyra pushed full steam ahead on her reality TV shows. In 2007, embarking on cycle nine of *America's Next Top Model*, Tyra showed no signs that she'd be slowing down soon. Her talk show, which had been nominated for six Daytime Emmy Awards, launched its third season, and Tyra planned to continue to wear the producer hat as she prepared to star in an upcoming feature film. Her company also had five shows in varying stages of production, including a sitcom and a one-hour drama. In addition, Tyra had created a licensing firm that she planned to use to market her own line of lingerie. Finally, Tyra was also looking to launch an online company.[9]

AMERICA'S NEXT TOP WADDLE

Things were rolling along just fine until Tyra's bod got some undesired media attention in early 2007. On her hit show, *America's Next Top Model*, Tyra has always stressed the importance of body confidence. But when the 33-year-old was enjoying a holiday in Australia, she was photographed in a bathing suit on the beach with a fuller frame by Australian tabloids. They ran the photos under headlines that blared, "America's Next Top Waddle," and "Tyra Porkchops."[10]

Tyra admitted to her talk show audience that she had put on 30 pounds since her modeling career began and now weighed a healthy 161 pounds, but the Australian tabloid claimed she'd gained 40 pounds. Tyra responded to the media with her typical chutzpa. Instead of hiding out or denying the charges, she decided to fight back. "I Googled myself," she told *Cosmopolitan* magazine, confessing she was upset with what she found. "I read positive things as well as letters from haters, so I don't do it anymore. I will say I'd rather the tabloids call me fat than a woman who is struggling. Women were saying, 'Tyra, if they call you fat, I must be a whale.' So I'll take the bullet for the girls out there."[11]

TYRA FIGHTS BACK

Despite the media circus of negative buzz, Tyra was not about to give the press the satisfaction of seeing her crumble. "When the going gets tough, the tough get back in their bathing suits," she told Diane Sawyer, host of the morning talk show, *Good Morning America*. Tyra told Diane that instead of hiding out from the press, she planned to retaliate by climbing into her bathing suit for her talk show, "dimples in my booty" and all. "Every night I wake up at 3 a.m. in the morning and think about the response," Tyra told Diane. "The show and the photo shoot are not just a fight against tabloids but a fight for women."[12]

KISS MY FAT ASS!

Tyra also appeared on the cover of *People* magazine in a swimsuit and gave them an exclusive interview, elaborating on her much-buzzed-about weight gain. "I get so much mail from young girls who say, 'I look up to you, you're not as skinny as everyone else, I think you're beautiful,'" she says. "So when they say that my body is 'ugly' and 'disgusting,' what does that make those girls feel like?" Tyra told *People* she currently weighed 161 pounds, or about 30 more than when she graced the cover of the *Sports Illustrated* Swimsuit Issue in 1997. "I still feel hot, but every day is different," she admitted. "It's when I put on the jeans that used to fit a year ago and don't fit now and give me the muffin top, that's when I say, 'Damn!'" In her defense, Tyra told *People* that photos were taken at an unflattering angle to make her appear even heavier that she was.[13]

According to *People* editor Larry Jackett, while Tyra was initially shy about showing off her flab, when she heard about all the letters the magazine had received in her defense, she changed her mind. "When *People* prepared to interview Tyra for the February 5 cover story of the magazine, they were told there was nothing about her body she wouldn't share . . . except for a glimpse of her posterior," writes Jackett.

> As she posed in a red leotard, Tyra asked everyone—even the photographer—to stand in front of her, later saying with a laugh, "No one sees my cellulite!" But that was before she started hearing from fans—*People* readers sent more than 300 letters and posted nearly 1,000 comments on people.com—who were inspired by the ex-model's proud admission that she now tips the scales at—gasp!—161 pounds. As she learned of how she had inspired countless women to love their bodies (the good, the bad, and the cellulite), Tyra decided it was time she did the same.[14]

TYRA BARES ALL ON HER TALK SHOW

Tyra decided to use her talk show for full disclosure. For an episode of *The Tyra Banks Show*, Tyra—and her entire audience—donned the red leotard, touting their weights. And this time Tyra allowed a 360-degree view. "I can't believe I'm letting you see this!" she exclaimed. Tyra then invited four women who had been moved by her story to share their epiphanies, like Louisville, Kentucky, nurse Tabitha Thomas, 23, who was considering taking diet pills even though she knew doing so could aggravate a heart defect. After reading Tyra's tale, "I thought, 'I just need to embrace this,'" Thomas said.[15]

SO WHAT?

Tyra said she hoped to help other women do the same: During the taping she announced her "So what?" campaign, which she described as "a movement that encourages women to say to ourselves, 'I'm not perfect—so what!'" Guest Mary Harrison, 25, caught on quickly enough. "My thighs jiggle when I walk," she told the audience. "And so what!" But Tyra's finest moment was when she told her audience about her hear-me-roar call. "All of you that have something nasty to say about me . . . [about] women who've been picked on, women whose husbands put them down . . . or girls in school. I have one thing to say to you: Kiss my fat ass!"[16]

Tyra later told *Shape* magazine that she had never shied away from discussing women's weight issues on her talk show. In fact, having her own weight put in the spotlight gave her the opportunity to speak about the issue from a personal view, in a way she never could before. "I was raised by women who don't believe that being super-skinny is the epitome of beauty," said Tyra. "Being the best that you can be? That's beautiful, and I wanted to find a way to encourage every woman to love her body. If I weigh 161 pounds or have cellulite on my butt, so what! I think I'm beautiful, and if you have a problem with that, so what!"

She added that strangers as well as celebrities were getting behind her crusade. "Women on the street yell out their weight to me," says Tyra. "And I was at a Hollywood party and Jennifer Hudson, Kirsten Dunst, even Leonardo DiCaprio came up to tell me that I was kicking butt. I was so proud of what we were doing!" Tyra said her talk show received thousands of emails and video testimonies from women about their weight, and the "So What!" movement has become so popular that Tyra's planning to produce more "So What!"-themed programs next season.[17]

TYRA'S UPS AND DOWNS

In a candid moment, Tyra confessed to *People* magazine that like everyone else, she's had her ups and downs when it comes to her weight and usually feels better when she's thinner. Since she retired from modeling in 2005, the number on the scale has fluctuated from 148–162 pounds, depending on how well she is taking care of herself. "I feel more comfortable when I'm lighter—I sleep better, I snore less, I have more endurance when I work out, my arms look better," she said, adding that she's not freaking out about wearing size 32-waist jeans or about "the fat roll" she claims to have on her back. Tyra said her biggest source of figure angst was her size-DD breasts, which she said made it hard to find clothes that fit. "I would love for them to be a size and a half smaller. But I've made millions of dollars with the body I have, so where's the pain in that? If I was in pain, I would have dieted. The pain is not there—the pain is someone printing a picture of me and saying those [horrible] things."[18]

Tyra added that her extra padding had one bright side—it seemed to add to her credibility as a talk show host. "[TV execs] think it's better when I'm at 155 lbs.—at 145, they feel I'm not as relatable," she told *People*. She also said she was having a lot more fun "eating the pancakes off a friend's plate at IHOP than trying to fit into designer sample sizes. Of course, if someone would come up with a miracle cure for cellulite, she's not above admitting she'd be first in line. "I think every woman would want to do something about their cellulite!"[19]

By May, just five months after photographs of her beachwear left her in tears, Tyra had shed 30 pounds. "With all the self-esteem my mom instilled in me, the criticism still hurts," she said.[20] Marcellas Reynolds, a frequent guest on *The Tyra Banks Show*, said her craft-service table "is now entirely absent of junk food and carbs. All you see are lean turkey sandwiches and loads of fresh-cut veggies and fruit."[21]

YOU WON'T REALLY BE AMERICA'S NEXT TOP MODEL

Meanwhile, Tyra's butt wasn't the target taking arrows from the press. In 2005, its fifth season still wildly popular and making Tyra richer by the day, *America's Next Top Model* started drawing fire from some in the media who believed the show was an elaborate hoax offering false hope to young girls, and that no matter who won the prize, she had no chance of ever becoming America's next top model.

"The truth at the core of this least-real reality series, now in its fifth season and with nearly five million viewers from the coveted demographic of women age 18 to 34, is that the winner is never Nikki or Kim or Nicole or Lisa. It is Tyra Banks, the show's host and producer, a Victoria's Secret beauty with a snap queen's attitude and the entrepreneurial chops of Donald Trump," wrote *The New York Times*.[22]

"What is not apparent to legions of modeling hopefuls, either on the show or out in TV land, is something that modeling business insiders tend to laugh about. In an industry that is indeed fairly cutthroat, the women who appear on *America's Next Top Model* would have a tough time wedging a flip-flop in the door of most agencies—and for several reasons. For starters most of them are too old to succeed in a field where much of the talent is recruited out of high school," according to Cathy Gould, the director of Elite models. Most are too plump to succeed in a business where models are expected to be model-thin. But the most serious strike against them is that they are American. According to James Scully, a famous casting agent, "Americans are just not in."[23]

In fact, if someone had asked who would become America's next top model five years ago, the answer would have been easy, according to the *New York Times*. "She was a Brazilian. The platoon of pillow-lipped and long-limbed beauties led by Gisele Bündchen appeared so abruptly on the scene that it seemed as though Brazil was some unknown planet suddenly discovered by astronomers combing the cosmic beauty-sphere. When the Brazilians' moment in the sun faded, those women were supplanted by Belgians, a raft of wan types with odd all-vowel names."[24]

TYRA'S GENDER-BENDING GUESTS

Tyra was also creating controversy on her talk show by inviting a series of unusual guests, many of whom had never appeared in the bright light of daytime TV. In October 2004, Tyra invited gay men and transgenders to compete on *America's Next Top Model*, a move that delighted *The Advocate*, the national gay and lesbian magazine, while irritating the mainstream media. According to *The Advocate*, Tyra's "transgender" episode was "the gayest moment on prime-time TV in 2004," and was "filled to the balm with perhaps the most flamboyant gay men ever to grace the public airwaves."[25]

Tyra's October 13 episode was timed to air the week of National Coming Out Day and featured everything from Paris Hilton stylists to top hair deisgners. Not that it was the first time a gay man had appeared on her show. As *The Advocate* pointed out, that honor belonged to "Miss" J. Alexander, an international model coach and runway walking expert who has been part of America's Next Top Model since the second episode of season 1."[26]

According to Ken Mok, coproducer of Top Model, giving a gay man a prominent role on the show had not been a publicity or ratings stunt but a deliberate attempt to portray the fashion industry. "Look, we are going to do a very accurate representation of the fashion world," he told The Advocate. "The reality is there are many people in the fashion world who are gay, and we are going to represent that on TV. We've not got[ten] any negative feedback. It's really, really weird. In fact, we continually get positive feedback on J. Alexander and the gay people who are on the show. That's truly surprising to me. It's got to be an honest show. And frankly, when you see J.'s legs, don't you want to see him like that? He's got great legs. If I had his legs, I would show them off."[27]

TRANSGENDER CONTESTANTS VIE FOR AMERICA'S NEXT TOP MODEL

In 2008, Tyra upped the ante and infuriated the Religious Right by inviting transgender Isis King on her show to compete for the title of America's Next Top Model. As a little boy in the Washington suburbs, Darrell Walls liked to pretend to be Lil' Kim or a Pink Power Ranger. He felt different—like a girl mistakenly born a boy. The casting of Isis on Tyra's show gave audiences a chance to see how the very slender, long-legged King fared on photo shoots and before judges. It also treated them to behind-the-scenes comments from some of Isis's fellow contestants, including one who called her a man and another who made a "drag queen" reference.[28] Viewers also got a glimpse of how Isis was transitioning from man to woman; in one episode, Isis injected female hormones. In a later show, Tyra told Isis that she would pay for the necessary surgery to turn him into a woman. "I don't believe the surgery will make me any more of a woman," replied Isis, who had been living as a woman for more than a year. "I've always been that woman. But it's something I feel will complete me."

While King's dreams of being America's Next Top Model bit the dust when he was booted off the show in September, after Tyra and her three fellow judges "decided Isis had to go after too many uninspiring photo shoots and catwalk sessions," Tyra later made good on her promise to make him a real woman.[29]

In November 2008, Tyra invited Isis on her talk show, where she surprised him by offering to pay for his sex-change operation. On the show, Tyra introduced Isis to Dr. Marci Bowers, a leading gender reassignment surgeon who had undergone the surgery himself to become a woman. When Isis said he couldn't afford to pay for the pricey surgery, Dr. Bowers offered to pay for it herself.[30]

SOME WEREN'T SO GLAAD

Tyra was commended for her "courageous stance towards gays and transgenders" by GLAAD, the Gay and Lesbian Alliance Against Defamation, who honored her with a 2008 GLAAD AWARD for her fair and accurate representations of the lesbian, gay, bisexual, and transgender community.[31]

But some in the mainstream media were less impressed with Tyra and questioned her values, if not her motives. "While other celebrities are busy throwing their money behind charities that feed the hungry, or put an end to violence in far-off lands, Tyra Banks clearly has her pulse on the issues that really matter—which is why Banks, the host of *America's Next Top Model*, has found a doctor to perform pro bono sexual reassignment surgery for Isis King, the first transgender contestant on *Top Model*," reported *Actress Achives*. "So everybody wins. King gets her surgery and Tyra Banks gets her name in the paper for taking on a cause nobody else would ever care about."[32]

Others wondered if Tyra had simply done it as a publicity stunt to pump up her ratings. "With 10 cycles under its size-zero belt, *America's Next Top Model* makes an attempt at reinvention in the 11th cycle of the series," wrote *The Post-Standard* in Syracuse, New York.

> Naming a full-figured person as the winner of cycle 10, the show tries to break ground and make a statement, carrying this on through the current season. Tyra Banks has always been outspoken—annoying, in fact. But is *America's Next Top Model* trying too hard? The short answer is yes. For the first time in the show's history, a transgender individual is competing for top honors. I can't help but think that this twist in the competition is

a further stab at attracting viewers. *America's Next Top Model* may need to take its final catwalk.[33]

"YOU'RE FIRED!"

Meanwhile, the arrows weren't just coming from the media. Tyra was also being attacked by people who had been on the show, either as contestants or judges. One of her most vocal detractors was former judge and supermodel Janice Dickinson, whom Tyra had canned a few years back for being too mean to the girls. Appearing in June 2009 on the *American Idol* finale, Dickinson slammed Tyra for firing former judge Paulina Porizkova and insinuated that Tyra was a liar and opportunist. "That's how Tyra rolls. Tyra rolls like that. She likes to fire people just about when she's promising them large amounts of money, then they get the ax, like I did. And then she takes the money and runs."[34]

NOTES

1. Lynn Hirschberg, "Banksable," *New York Times Magazine*, June 1, 2008.

2. Ibid.

3. Quoted by Lila Chase, *Totally Tyra: An Unauthorized Biography* (New York: Penguin Group, 2006), 75.

4. Samantha Critchell, "Tyra Banks Takes Final Spin on the Runway," *AP Online*, December 5, 2005, www.highbeam.com/doc/1P1-115885472.html.

5. Quoted by Kiri Blakely. "Tyra Banks on It," *Forbes* (July 2001), www.forbes.com/free_forbes/2006/0703/120.html (accessed May 15, 2009).

6. Holly More Eagleson, "Fun Fearless Phenoms 2008: When You're Stressing about How to Pull Off Your Big Dreams, It Helps to Seek Out Chicks Who've Found Fame and Success," *Cosmopolitan*, September 1, 2008, www.cosmopolitan.com/.../Fun-Fearless-Phenom-Awards (accessed June 14, 2009).

7. Ibid.

8. Quoted by Eagleson, "Fun Fearless Phenoms 2008."

9. Hirschberg, "Banksable."

10. "Banks Mortified by Mean-Spirited Tabloid Reports," *WENN News*, January 29, 2007, www.wenn.com (accessed June 20, 2009).

11. Quoted by Eagleson, "Fun Fearless Phenoms 2008."

12. "Tyra Banks Fights Back Against Tabloid Fat Allegations," *Good Morning America*, January 31, 2007, www.abcnews.go.com/GMA/ (accessed June 20, 2009).

13. Quoted by Allison Adato, "Tyra Talks," *People* 67 (February 5, 2007): 82, www.people.com/people/archive/article/0,,20062626,00.html (accessed June 21, 2009).

14. Larry Jackett, "Inside People," *People*, March 5, 2007, www.people.com (accessed June 21, 2009).

15. The Tyra Banks Show, http://tyrashow.warnerbros.com (accessed June 21, 2009).

16. Quoted by Adato, "Tyra Talks."

17. Quoted by Claire Connors. "Why I Love My Body . . . Just the Way It Is," *Shape*, June 1, 2007, www.shape.com (accessed June 21, 2009).

18. Quoted by Adato, "Tyra Talks."

19. Ibid.

20. "Tyra Banks Sheds 30 Pounds in Five Months," May 23, 2007, www.theinsider.com/news/188859_Tyra_Banks_Sheds_30_Pounds_In_Five_Months.

21. Ibid.

22. Guy Trebay, "Who Is America's Next Top Model, Really?" *The New York Times*, November 6, 2005, www.nytimes.com/2005/11/06/fashion/sundaystyles/06model.html?_r=1&scp=1&sq=Who%20Is%20America's%20Next%20Top%20Model,%20Really&st=cse (accessed June 22, 2009).

23. Ibid.

24. Ibid.

25. Adam B. Vary, "America's Next Top Role Models: The Courageous and Outrageous Queens of *America's Next Top Model* Are More

Than Ready for Prime Time,"*The Advocate*, January 18, 2005, www.highbeam.com/doc/1G1-126792432.html (accessed June 23, 2009).

26. *America's Next Top Model*, www.cwtv.com/shows/americas-next-top-model (accessed June 22, 2009).

27. Gillian Gaynair, "A New Twist for *America's Next Top Model*," *AP Worldstream*, September 26, 2008, www.highbeam.com/doc/1A1-D93E21502.html (accessed June 23, 2009).

28. "Names and Faces," *Washington Post*, September 27, 2008, www.washingtonpost.com (accessed June 22, 2009).

29. "Tyra Surprises Isis with Sex Change Operation," *Hollyscoop.com*, November 17, 2008, www.hollyscoop.com/tv/tyra-banks/tyra-surprises-isis-with-sex-change-operation_1396.aspx (accessed June 23, 2009).

30. Ibid.

31. Julie Lipson, "GLAAD Awards Honors Media in San Francisco," *LA's the Place.com*, May 8, 2008, http://lastheplace.com/2008/05/08/glaad-awards-honors-media-in-san-francisco.

32. Shallon Lester, "Tyra Banks Gives 'Top Model' Contestant Isis Sex-Change Surgery Gift," *New York Daily News*, November 17, 2009, www.nydailynews.com/gossip/2008/11/17/2008-11-17_tyra_banks_gives_top_model_contestant_is.html.

33. "TV Critics Corner," *The Post Standard* (Syracuse, NY), September 21, 2008, www.post-standard.com.

34. Quoted by Jocelyn Bera, "Janice Dickinson Slams Tyra Banks Over Paulina Porizkova Firing," *WENN News*, May 22, 2009, www.imdb.com/name/nm0596298/news (accessed June 4, 2009).

Chapter 7

TYRA BECOMES A MEDIA MOGUL

In 2003, Tyra became a true pioneer in reality TV when she created, executive produced, and hosted the tremendously successful *America's Next Top Model*. The show quickly became a phenomenon and was UPN's most-watched program for six cycles. In 2006, *Top Model* was chosen to launch the brand new CW network. The premiere was the best ever in the 18–34 demographic and one of the largest viewing audiences in the show's history. *Top Model* continued to be a hit internationally, with the American edition appearing in more than 100 countries, with an additional 20 countries adapting their own version. By 2008, the show had celebrated its 110th cycle, and in February 2008 aired its 100th episode. With the launch of her syndicated daily talk show, *The Tyra Banks Show*, Tyra became one of only a few women to be seen regularly on both daytime and nighttime television. The efforts of Tyra and her talk show crew were validated in June 2008, when *The Tyra Banks Show* won the Daytime Emmy Award for Talk Show, Informative—the first talk show to ever be awarded in this new category.[1]

TYRA BRANCHES OUT

Although Tyra had her hands full with two reality TV shows, she wasn't content to sit on her laurels—or any other part of her anatomy!

In 2007, Tyra signed a long-term production deal with Warner Bros. to develop scripted shows, reality fare, movies, and straight-to-DVD projects. "I want to create shows that attract my core audience and that are aspirational and empowering. But we're going to have a lot of fun with those messages, too. Warner Bros. understands my brand and the reach and demand of our audience," she told *Variety* magazine.[2]

In November 2008, Tyra introduced her first movie as an executive producer. *The Clique*, a direct-to-DVD movie, is based on *The New York Times* best-selling teen novel series of the same name which has sold millions of copies and spent nearly 100 weeks on the *New York Times* best-seller's list. Tyra's movie, like the books, explores the highs and lows of junior high life through the eyes of an elite group of socially precocious 12-year-old girls from the wealthy New York suburbs.[3]

Tyra told *ET Online* that she decided to produce *The Clique* because she identified with it herself. "I identify with 'The Clique' personally, because I've been on both sides. I've been the queen bee, and I've been the girl that wants to be in it so badly, but is just so awkward and never will be."[4]

DESPERATELY SEEKING STYLISTA

Tyra also began casting around for other ways to flex her skills as executive producer for a TV reality show series, telling *Newsweek* that being a producer was more up her alley than modeling had ever been.[5] "Actresses or singers travel with entourages, with their hair and makeup people and tour managers. Models are alone. Even when you're the biggest supermodel in the world, you're alone," she said. "At the age of 32, I decided I didn't want to be like those boxers who continue to get beat up and say they're going to retire, but they don't, and then their legacy is marred. I wanted to leave on top."[6]

But Tyra emphasized that she had no plans of leaving behind what she had learned and accomplished from her years in the modeling industry. She told *Newsweek* she planned to tap into her "glory in the modeling world and use the power I have now to cultivate new talent in front of the camera and behind the scenes. If you have entrepreneurial dreams, you have to live it and breathe it. You have to treat the idea like a baby, like your child. You don't sleep when you have a new baby."[7]

Tyra had seen the immensely popular Hollywood movie *The Devil Wears Prada*, starring Meryl Streep and Anne Hathaway, and thought she could create a reality competition show that would recreate the humor, rivalry, and tension of working at a major fashion magazine portrayed in the movie (which was based on a book by the same name). Although the movie and book were loosely modeled on working under *Vogue* magazine editor-in-chief Anna Wintour, renowned for her demanding and catty nature, Tyra decided to base her reality show on the fashion magazine *Elle*. The result was *Stylista*, a reality competition series for aspiring fashion magazine editors that debuted on October 29, 2008, on The CW network.[8]

Elle fashion news editor Anne Slowey and the magazine's creative director, Joe Zee, were tapped by Tyra to serve as the show's mentors, with Slowey responsible for eliminating a contestant each week. Slowey had previously appeared on Heidi Klum's *Project Runway* as a guest judge, so she already had some experience as a judge.[9]

Billed as *The Devil Wears Prada* reinvented as a reality series, the show pitted 11 young fashion enthusiasts against a variety of challenges they would need to master in order to work on a fashion magazine—from fetching coffee and buying the perfect breakfast for their boss, to creating award-winning outfits on a dime-store budget. The show ran for eight episodes, with the grand-prize winner receiving a paid, yearlong *Elle* editorial position, a paid lease on a Manhattan apartment for a year, and a $100,000 clothing allowance at H&M (a popular clothing store chain).[10]

TV'S NEW "MEANIE"

After one episode, media wags claimed Slowey was making the devil look like a saint. When interviewed by reporters appalled by the insults and humiliation she heaped on the show's contestants, she responded in a Devil-Wears-Prada fashion, telling reporters that two decades of experience in the fashion industry had given her license to come down hard on the newbies. "My first day at *Vogue*, I had to go out and buy 32 goldfish and put them in 32 bowls and transport them to this woman's house without killing any of them," she said, as a way of defending her-self. "I've had the privilege to become very eccentric and very picky. And I get very particular about my coffee. I have trained staffs in hotels in Paris and Milan to get it right. Some people think I'm a little nuts, but I like things the way I like them."[11]

In fact, while the show was filmed at a fake Elle office in Soho (Tyra and Mok didn't think the magazine's real headquarters in midtown Manhattan were swank enough), Slowey insisted she was not playing a character. "I'm just being myself," she told the *New York Post*, dis-missing charges that she was rude or disrespectful to her underlings. "People perceive honest as mean and it is not. I imagine at the White House, they have their own way of speaking to each other which some-body working at a not-for-profit eco fund might find abrupt. It is hard to judge people when you are not on the inside."

When pressed, Slowey admitted she probably got away with her "diva" attitude because she rarely ventured outside the cocoon of the fashion world, where her power was seldom questioned. "My life is my work, my work is my life," she says. "Most of my friends are from the industry, so it is hard to distinguish the difference."[12]

STYLISTA STUNG BY TV CRITICS

While *America's Next Top Model*, now in it fourth season, was still outperforming other shows in its time slot, and Tyra's talk show had been awarded for a daytime Emmy, *Stylista* was another story entirely. From the first episode on, it was clear that *Stylista* was not bound for glory—or even another season. Even media moguls who claimed they loved the show confessed they didn't think it was in the same league as Tyra's other two reality TV shows, and pointed to the show's dire ratings as proof.

"The CW's Stylista has been on for a few weeks now and from a critical perspective (that is, ours), the show is kind of genius. So why doesn't it have the ratings to match?" wrote the *New York Observer*.

The show has all the requisite reality show ingredients: The bitchy Megan has more personality in one strand of her stringy hair than all of the current contestants on *America's Next Top Model* combined. The 20-year-old NYU journalism girl, Devin (who thought she had the fashion magazine world figured out because she edited the school fashion magazine for some time), sadly reminds us of the way we were coming out of the very same institution. And we even can't help but find the character with the unfortunate nickname of "Boobs" sort of endearing. Then there is Anne Slowey, the *Elle* fashion editor that we expected to be a nightmare, but who actually turned out to be refreshingly candid and pleasant off-camera. Like the time she admitted to us that fashion is sort of an absurd and ridiculous industry—so true! Or the time she told us that she's been wearing the same pair of leggings and a tank top in her office every day for the past two and a half weeks in protest of the heat being turned up.[13]

But the Observer admitted the ratings for the show "just haven't caught up with our overall enthusiasm about it." According to Nielsen, the show was getting just a measly two million viewers compared to *America's Next Top Model's* four million.[14]

"A CHEAP KNOCKOFF"

And that was the good review! Other newspapers were far less generous in their praise for *Stylista*, calling it everything from "mean-spirited" and "shallow" to "a cheap knockoff of her other reality shows."

"Stitched with meanness, zealousness and a flair of despair, CW's *Stylista* seeks to trick you into thinking it's an original. It's really just a knockoff of any number of other reality shows," wrote the *Boston Herald*. "In this unpleasant competition, fashion-setters vie for a one-year junior editor position at Elle magazine. The casting directors have done their jobs well. This crew is a crate of fireworks waiting for a match. This show is satisfied with stripping away dignity."[15] *The Herald* also panned the caliber of the acting, in particular, Slowey's cloning of Meryl Streep in *The Devil Wears Prada*. "Slowey makes an entrance that proves she's watched *The Devil Wears Prada* at least a dozen times. It would be laughable were it not so poorly executed."[16]

But they saved their fiercest criticism for Tyra. "Much like her never-ending *America's Next Top Model*, the show's emphasis is on contemptible behavior," the paper said. "Cast mates almost immediately strategize to neutralize others. Megan has something nasty to say about everyone. One contestant has several meltdowns over being forced to wear clothes that cover her expensive cleavage. The personal dramas rage out of control next week, leading one contestant to collapse in the throes of a panic attack. Instead of frocks, the cast is judged on their page layouts. It may be appropriate for their would-be careers, but it makes for tedious TV."[17]

The *Washington Post* chimed in with a scalding article that not only dismissed the notion that anyone would ever want to be a stylista, but criticized the show as nasty, uninspired, and unoriginal. "Not only is there really no such thing as a stylista, but also neither should there be," the paper said.

> Nobody should want such a person to exist, and certainly nobody should aspire to be one. We have entered a hyperventilated universe in which all that matters is appearance, although contestants are told that to succeed at a fashion magazine, they must also be prepared "to live and breathe style." It's doubtful any of the contestants, all in their boring 20s, would list "Peace Corps worker" or "community organizer" as a second choice of occupation. But logic, propriety and what I like playfully to call simple human decency are no obstacles.[18]

Calling *Stylist* a copycat, *The Post* also criticized the show for aping the structure of Donald Trump's *The Apprentice* while attempting to mine the same old lode as other reality shows set in the fashion world, Tyra's *America's Next Top Model* among them. "*Stylista*" is like a little tick that you want to flick off, but it's no worse than other reality games that have come before and will come after. It celebrates and elevates life's most trivial drivel, but if that were a crime, reality television would quickly go the way of the crooked quiz shows of the '50's."[19]

Adding insult to injury, fashion insiders at *New York Magazine* said *Stylista* had totally missed the mark by trying to substitute *Elle* magazine's Anne Slowey for the powerful and all-mighty Anna Wintour of *Vogue*, as portrayed in *The Devil Wears Prada*.

> Anne's icy demeanor is blatantly imitative of Meryl Streep's in the film, and even the cruel intonation and (less entertaining) phrasing is similar. Which makes sense for producers who may want to cash in on the excitement people had for the movie. But the problem is, Meryl's

character was based on Anna Wintour, the most powerful woman at the most powerful magazine in fashion. And Anne Slowey, for all her talents, is not the most powerful woman at a magazine that is not the most powerful one in fashion. For her to imitate Meryl-imitating-Anna feels embarrassing. It highlights in a painfully obvious way how desperately *Elle* wants to be *Vogue*. And it's uncomfortable.[20]

TRUE BEAUTY IS ONLY SKIN DEEP

When *Stylista* wrapped at the end of December (given the low ratings, it's no surprise the show did not have a second season), Tyra, undaunted, decided to try her luck producing another new reality TV show called *True Beauty*. The show, which debuted in January 2009, was a beauty competition with a twist: Ten attractive contestants thought they were vying to be named the most physically beautiful person, but they were, unbeknownst to them, also being judged on their inner beauty, behaviors and kindness, among other criteria.[21]

Vanessa Minnillo, a one-time Miss Teen USA and the host of the show along with three other judges, including Nole Marin and Cherly Tieggs, told *TV Guide* that she signed on for the seven-episode show in the hopes it would have a ripple effect "and make people think twice about what they say or how they act or how they treat others." Fat chance of that! Each week's show revolved around what Minnillo called "a covert and an overt challenge. We have a challenge that they know about that is aesthetically based and in that challenge, we have hidden challenges. So if we send them out into the world to do a challenge based on just physical beauty, we're actually looking at their insides and we test them on honesty, kindness, graciousness, humility as well as whatever the physical challenge is." As Minnillo told *TV Guide*, true beauty wasn't just about outer beauty but inner beauty as well. "I'll be the first one to tell you I wasn't the most beautiful girl there."[22]

Unfortunately, the show didn't seem to bring out the true inner beauty of the contestants, Minnillo complained to *TV Guide*. "I was like, I can't believe a person, knowing that there's a camera, would actually say that. We're judging their inner beauty and their outer beauty, but they don't know that. In a hidden camera situation, I get it, like if they acted a certain way, I get it. But when they were sitting there full-on looking at the camera saying what they were saying, I couldn't believe it. I'm like, you're not even trying to be fake. You're just full-on: 'I'm hot! I'm a 10!'" Millillo told *TV Guide* that even after some of the contestants had figured out the show was rating them on their inner as well as outer beauty, "they were still were the same way, which blew my mind!"[23]

Minnillo attributed some of the contestants' rude, cocky behavior to "the world that they live in. For the first time, these kids who've never left their hometowns of, like, Idaho, are out in L.A. and we're giving them a reality check. I think some of them are like, 'Gosh, I'm not all that I thought I was.' But some of them are just like, 'Whatever. I'll just go home and be all that and a bag of chips!'"[24] Unlike the contestants on the show, Minnillo said she had been raised with a father who emphasized humility and who never hesitated to put her in her place. "He'd be the first one to put you in place and to tell you, 'Get up and get your own soda, don't ask someone to get it for you, be grateful for what you have, count your blessings,' and 'you put your pants on one leg at a time, just like everyone else,'" she told *TV Guide*. "But if you surround yourself with a lot of 'yes men,' then you have a different perception of yourself and the world."[25]

True Beauty, like *Stylista*, was skewered by television critics as superficial and pandering. "If beauty is only skin deep, where are all of the ugly people?" asked Ray Richmond, with *TV Review.com*. "This show, which in fairness also spreads the blame to Tyra Banks and her Bankable Production gang, feels very much like a reality show parody until you come to the stunning realization that everybody is—against all reason—entirely serious."[26]

According to *TV Review*, the plot revolves around "six gratingly earnest gorgeous babes and four cloyingly narcissistic hunky dudes" who lived together in an LA mansion, where they attempt to successfully bond. "The threadbare gimmick involved attempting to push beyond the shallow cosmetic sheen that drives these unscripted doltfests to uncover the 'inner beauty' of the contestants, which host/judge Vanessa Minnillo repeatedly assures is what's really important. The judges clandestinely judged everyone's character based on capturing selfish, boorish or insecure acts on hidden camera. If they fail to open a door for a guy carrying coffee, they're deemed pond scum."[27]

In the end, the show failed to live up to its promise to honor inner beauty, concluded *TV Review*.

> The woman sent packing at the end of the first episode is less than pleased to be labeled a hopeless bitch with an imperfect jawline. What's utterly disingenuous about this show is its banal insistence on being a measure of spirit, merit and decency when that's so clearly a joke. I'd have much more respect for *True Beauty* if it were to accept its limitations as a vainglorious orgy of inconsequence. But perhaps the biggest irony of the show was that the winner of the grueling assessment of body and soul received an undisclosed cash prize and a spot in *People* magazine's 100 Most Beautiful People issue![28]

Needless to say, with reviews like this, audiences quickly tuned out. When the first season of *True Beauty* ended, the show followed in the footsteps of *Stylista*, which is to say it completely vanished and was never heard from again.

THE YEAR OF AWARDS

Fortunately, the negative reviews of *Stylista* and *True Beauty* didn't seem to make a lasting dent in Tyra's reputation (to the surprise of many reviewers, who were hoping for a slow fade). Between 2007 and 2008, Tyra was named to countless lists of the most influential people, most beautiful people, top earners, hardest working celebrities, and so on—leaving Tyra's critics wondering if they had missed something.

In 2007, Tyra was one of *Time* magazine's most 100 influential people of the year, sharing the honor with such luminaries as heartthrob Leonardo DiCaprio and envelope-pushers Rosie O'Donnell, director Martin Scorsese, fellow model Kate Moss, and prominent politicians Hilary Clinton, Barak Obama, and Queen Elizabeth II. Other entertainers on the list included Tyra's mentor, Oprah Winfrey, as well as George Clooney, Brad Pitt, Justin Timberlake, Cate Blanchett, Tina Fey, Brian Williams, Michael J. Fox, California Governor Arnold Schwarzenegger, and *American Idol* creator Simon Fuller.[29] In 2007, Tyra was also saluted as a trailblazer and received a BET Honors award for her work in media alongside Time Warner CEO Richard Parsons and other notables. In 2005, *Forbes* profiled her on their highly anticipated "Celebrity 100" report for the first time.[30]

In 2008, Tyra won a Daytime Emmy for "Outstanding Talk Show/ Informative." As Tyra accepted the trophy, she paid tribute to the mentor who had given her the training and inspiration for the reality talk show host gig. "I want to thank Oprah Winfrey for her inspiration," Tyra said. "She is the queen. She will always be the queen."[31] Tyra was also honored by *Cosmopolitan* as one of the magazine's 2008 "Fun Fearless Phenom" award winners. Tyra told *The Insider*, "I feel I am more goofy and crazy and out there. As for [the] fearless part, I am full of fear, but I think the fearless part is pushing past the fear," she said, explaining that she was afraid of dolphins and whales but fearless when it came to telling people how much she now weighed.[32]

In spring 2008, Tyra appeared on the cover of the *New York Times Magazine* in a piece titled "Martha, Oprah, Tyra; Is She the Next Big Female Branded Self?" and *Entertainment Weekly* featured her on the cover saying "America's Next Top Mogul." In the same year, she was also honored in *Hollywood Reporter's* "100 Most Powerful Women in Entertainment," *Entertainment Weekly's* "25 Smartest in Television," and *Glamour* magazine's coveted "Women of the Year."[33] Nobody in the entertainment world was surprised when Tyra was named the Hardest-Working Celebrity in Show Business by a *Parade* magazine poll in July 2008.[34]

TYRA EARNS BIG BUCKS

Tyra's tireless efforts were also doing wonders for her bank account. In June 2008, Tyra topped the list of *Forbes* magazine's "Primetime TV's Top Earning Women," earning a reported $28 million, followed by fellow supermodel Heidi Klum, host of *Project Runway*, earning a reported $14 million for her role as host. Tyra was also number 68 on *Forbes's* list of top-earners.[35]

When *Ebony* magazine interviewed her about her top-earning power, Tyra told them her fat bank account was partly due to her not liking to spend money—a fact *Ebony* found surprising considering she had just bought her father an expensive house.[36]

But Tyra said when it came to spending money, she was "all about value. For instance, I'm decorating a new apartment in New York right now, and I have a meeting with the designer and I'm going to tell him, 'I don't care how much money they say I make in a year. It could be more, it could be less. But you don't need to be looking at that number and spending my money as if it is yours.'" She told the magazine she also saved money by staying with her mom when she's in Los Angeles; by making presents for her senior staffers; and, for her New York offices, by choosing to paint the walls rather than change the carpeting because she felt new paint is more affordable than new carpeting.[37]

While Tyra admitted to being thrifty, she emphasized she was not a tightwad or cheap when it came to rewarding employees and giving big tips. In 2008, Tyra decided to skip her annual out-of-country Christmas holiday trip so she could pocket the cash and give it to her employees. "I gotta take care of my people," she told *Ebony*. "Hotel prices are at a peak. Because of what's going on with the economy I've decided not to take that vacation. So I was like, I'll just chill. I'm doing a 'stay-cation.'"[38]

NOTES

1. Tyra Banks Website, www.tyrabanks.com (accessed June 20. 2009).

2. Josef Adalian, "Warner Expands Tyra Banks Deal; Host Signs Multiyear Pact with Studio," *Variety*, October 29, 2007, www .variety.com/article/VR1117974950.html?categoryid=1236&cs=1 (accessed June 9, 2009).

3. Ibid.

4. "Exclusive: On 'The Clique' Set with Tyra Banks!" *ETOnline.com*, February 29, 2008, www.etonline.com/news/2008/02/ 59136 (accessed June 13, 2009).

5. Tyra Banks, "An Empire Behind the Scenes," *Newsweek*, October 13, 2008, www.newsweek.com/id/162338 (accessed June 24, 2009).

6. Ibid.

7. Ibid.

8. "Exclusive: On 'The Clique' Set with Tyra Banks!"

9. Ibid.

10. Adalian, "Warner Expands Tyra Banks Deal."

11. Sean Daly, "Reality TV's New Meanie Elle-ish Fashion Boss Brings Devil to Life," *New York Post*, July 21, 2008.

12. Ibid.

13. Irina Aleksander, "*Stylista* Ratings Not Meeting Our Great Expectations," *New York Observer*, November 13, 2008, www.observer.com/2008/o2/stylista-ratings-not-meeting-our-great-expectations (accessed June 24, 2009).

14. Ibid.

15. Mark A. Perigard, "Cheap Knockoff: CW Reality Series 'Stylista' Simply Wears on You," *Boston Herald*, October 22, 2008, www.bostonherald.com/entertainment/television/reviews/view.bg?articleid=1126961 (accessed June 24, 2008).

16. Ibid.

17. Ibid.

18. Tom Shales, "Stylista Reality Right Off the Rack," *Washington Post*, October 22, 2008, www.washingtonpost.com (accessed June 24, 2009).

19. Ibid.

20. Chris Rovsar, "Why We're Embarrassed for *Elle*, Anne Slowey, and *Stylista*," *New York Magazine*, May 14, 2008, http://nymag.com/daily/fashion/2008/05/why_we_are_embarrassed_for_ann.html (accessed June 24. 2009).

21. Joyce Eng, "Vanessa Minnillo Finds the *Beauty* Within," *TV Guide*, January 1, 2009, www.tvguide.com/news/vanessa-minnillo-previews-1001218.aspx (accessed June 25, 2009).

22. Ibid.

23. Ibid.

24. Ibid.

25. Ibid.

26. Ray Richmond, "True Beauty—TV Review," *TV Review*, January 6, 2009, www.hollywoodreporter.com/hr/tv-reviews/true-beauty-tv-review-1003927235.story (accessed June 25, 2009).

27. Ibid.

28. Ibid.

29. Heidi Klum, "The People Who Shape Our World," *Time*, www.time.com/time/magazine/article/0,9171,1187401,00.html.

30. www.tyrabanks.com (accessed June 29, 2009).

31. Derrik J. Lang, " 'Guiding Light,' Tyra Banks Wins Kick Off Daytime Emmys," *AP Online*, June 21, 2008, www.highbeam.com/doc/1A1-D91E4RN00.html (accessed June 29, 2009).

32. Victoria Recano, "The Insider Goes One-on-One with Tyra Banks," September 16, 2008, *The Insider News.com*, www.theinsidernews.com (accessed June 30, 2009).

33. www.tyrabanks.com (accessed June 29, 2009).

34. "Tyra Banks: Hardest Working Person in Showbiz," *Hollyscoop.com*, July 15, 2008, www.hollyscoop.com/tyra-banks/tyra-banks-hardest-working-person-in-showbiz_16849.aspx.

35. Lacey Rose, "Prime-Time TV's 20 Top-Earning Women," *Forbes*, September 2, 2008, www.forbes.com/2008/08/28/television-actresses-hollywood-biz-media-cx_lr_0902tvstars.html (accessed June 30, 2008).

36. Adrienne P. Samuels, "Tyra Unexpected: Smart but Not Cheap, Tyra Banks Swears She's Just and Ordinary Lady," *Ebony*, December 1, 2008, www.highbeam.com/doc/1G1-189551743.html (accessed June 30, 2009).

37. Ibid.

38. Ibid.

Chapter 8

FALSE NOTES, DEAD ENDS, AND BAD HAIR DAYS

Tyra hasn't always been a superstar, and just because she's rich and famous doesn't mean she hasn't had bad days like everyone else. In fact, Tyra claims overcoming the roadblocks and rejections in her career taught her to persevere despite all odds, and helped her get where she is today. After a career as a supermodel, actress, and even a brief fling at a singing career that went nowhere fast, Tyra has become one of the most highly paid women in Hollywood by discovering what she loves to do most, perfecting it, and sticking with it. While Tyra eventually found her true calling as a reality show producer and host, she had to try and fail (or at least not wildly succeed) at many other ventures before doing so.

SUCCESS AFTER A STRING OF FAILURES

As she told *Forbes* magazine in 2006, she came to her current success only after trying modeling, guest-starring on sitcoms, and giving a few stilted turns in such big-screen turkeys as Jerry Bruckheimer's *Coyote Ugly*. Then she tried to make herself into the next Mariah Carey, to no avail. In 2003, while she was still modeling, Tyra hired Carey's music manager Benny Medina, who had also worked with Jennifer Lopez, to help her perfect her singing voice for her first (and only) single, "Shake Ya Body." Tyra debuted the song on *America's Next Top*

Model. Despite the fact it was the most downloaded item on the UPN Web site, Tyra knew in her gut that she didn't have a strong enough voice to propel her into a successful singing career. Having learned that it was better to stick with what she did best rather than waste time and money on things she only did OK, she decided to abandon all thoughts of a singing career after making that one video. "Oh child, that was a dream," she told *Forbes.* "I sounded decent, but you shouldn't ever do something just because you're only decent at it."[1]

A LESS THAN PERFECT BOD

Having a less-than-stellar singing voice wasn't the only challenge Tyra faced in her career. She was also widely criticized for gaining 30 pounds after leaving the runway, and for having dimensions that no longer resembled a supermodel's. Tyra decided to use her après-runway weight gain and less-than-perfect proportions to debunk and demystify the modeling industry, decrying its unrealistic expectations of beauty and accompanying eating disorders and diet drug abuse. To-day, Tyra never misses a chance to reveal her flaws, whether it's show-ing off her cellulite, appearing on her talk show or in magazine shoots without makeup, or strolling around Los Angeles in a "fat suit" in an effort to demonstrate society's cruelty towards obese women.[2]

ROADBLOCKS IN MODELING

Like many black women trying to break into modeling in the late 1980s, Tyra also experienced her share of rejection, defeat, and humiliation as she went from one modeling agency to another in an effort to get someone to hire her. At the time Tyra was first breaking into the modeling world, there were only a handful of black models who worked on a regular basis. While Iman and Naomi Campbell had made it, cosmetic companies were looking for "all-American" (translation: white) faces to represent their product lines. Agencies told her that they already had a black model and didn't need another one, or dismissed her after looking at her photos for less than a minute. One agency told her that she might have potential on the runway, but that she could forget about being a cover girl because "I don't feel that the camera likes your face." A receptionist at another modeling agency suggested that Tyra learn how to type because that's where she'd be after her search for a modeling agency had ended. Finally, she was taken on by L.A. Models, then, a year later, when she was approaching high school graduation, decided to switch to Elite Modeling agency in Los Angeles. Through Elite, Tyra was offered a one-year modeling gig in Paris—and the rest is history.[3]

In 1993, Tyra discussed the racism she had encountered in the modeling industry with *Cosmopolitan* magazine. "I've had bookers tell me, 'You've got light skin and green eyes. You're easy to sell.' " Tyra also told the magazine she had relaxed her hair and had hair extensions done "because that's what 'beautiful' is supposed to look like—and that's how I make my living."[4]

But success did not insulate Tyra from random acts of racism in everyday life. When she and a friend went to a New York City newsstand to purchase a magazine whose cover Tyra graced, the proprietor screamed at the two women and told them to get out of the store. When her friend pointed out the issue and Tyra's image, the store owner responded by saying, "I don't care. You all look alike!"[5]

BAD DAYS WITH NAOMI CAMPBELL

Tyra's curves and healthy attitude towards her weight weren't the only things that set her apart from the modeling pact. Unlike many of her peers, Tyra did not smoke, drink, experiment with drugs, engage in premarital sex, or enjoy hanging out. This behavior, or lack thereof, made for some very lonely days as a young model in Paris, where she was ridiculed and ostracized for refusing to be part of the crowd.

But the supermodel who made life most difficult for Tyra in Paris was Naomi Campbell, who had already made it as a black supermodel and was jealous of Tyra's raising fame. With her slightly Asian look, which she inherited from a Chinese grandmother, Naomi's unique beauty had catapulted her to the top of the modeling industry. Discovered when she was 15, by the time Tyra arrived in Paris Campbell had already appeared on the covers of countless fashion magazines, including *Vogue*, *Cosmopolitan*, and *Elle*, and was always in demand on the runways of North America and Europe. Campbell had also branched out into films and television, and had kicked off the famous "milk mustache" ads.[6] While Campbell was known to be temperamental and moody, because of her special beauty and elegance she was also the darling of photographers, who enthused that her amazing body made clothing come alive. When the fashion industry began calling Tyra "the next Naomi Campbell," Naomi became jealous and enraged, and through her influence even got Tyra barred from modeling in a Chanel show.

"It's very sad that the fashion business and press as well as certain other models can't accept that there can be more than one reigning black supermodel at a time," Tyra said years later, adding that unlike Naomi, she never felt the need to edge her out to remain successful.[7]

In fact, truth be known, when it came to black models, Tyra and Naomi were so different in looks and personality that there was no need for Naomi to feel threatened by Tyra. From the beginning, Tyra embraced her blackness and put her heart into breaking through racial barriers, not just for herself, but for all black women. "I have been fortunate in my career to be able to transcend long-standing barriers," she says in her book. "I hope and realize that my success is paving the way for other firsts to be achieved until there is no longer a need for distinction."[8]

Naomi, on the other hand, tried to distance herself from her race, claiming she wasn't interested in being categorized as a black model. Ironically, in her own way Naomi also helped erase the racial divisions in modeling by insisting that modeling agencies become color blind. "They used to call up asking for a beautiful white model or a beautiful black model. Now they just ask for a beautiful model. It just doesn't matter what color you are anymore. If I've had anything to do with that change, then I'm really proud."[9]

After a long-standing feud, Tyra decided in 2005 that she was tired of the antagonism between herself and Naomi. She invited her on her talk show so the two of them could publicly make up, which they did to the delight of the audience. But Tyra didn't miss the opportunity to tell Naomi that she hadn't appreciated her efforts to sabotage her as young model.[10]

ROADBLOCKS TO PRODUCING

Being black isn't the only bias Tyra has had to fight during her career. When she tried to create the sort of show she would personally watch after her stint as a youth correspondent for the *Oprah* show in 1999–2000, she found the industry wasn't ready to accept a former model as a television producer. "As a model, my roadblock was being black and curvy. As a producer, my roadblock was being a model," she told *Entertainment Weekly*.[11]

When Banks developed the idea for *America's Next Top Model*, she initially met with resistance and indifference. But she and executive producer Ken Mok eventually found the show a home on the new fledging broadcast network UPN. "We pitched it to Ghen Maynard at CBS, and he said, 'I'm [also] in charge of UPN and I think this could be a really good flagship for them. At first, our feelings were a little hurt. 'Why do we have to go to the smaller network,'" Tyra asked him. "Then he was talking about demos, and CBS is older. He brought it to UPN and I'm so happy he did because it was nice to be a big fish in a small pond."[12]

Dawn Ostroff, former entertainment president of UPN and current entertainment president of The CW, admits that listening to Tyra's idea "was kind of a courtesy. Many times people have ideas who haven't worked in television, and you always take the pitch because you never know where a hit can come from. Tyra totally understood how to entertain when she pitched the show."[13]

RACE AGAINST TIME

Meanwhile, UPN wanted to get the show on the air as fast as possible. With preproduction beginning in the fall of 2002 in New York City, Tyra only had a month to scour the nation for contestants and used radio interviews to spread the word. "We didn't know what we were doing," Tyra told *Entertainment Weekly*. For judges, she turned to old friends in the modeling industry and tapped Janice Dickinson, a fellow supermodel with a party girl rep who later caused Tyra a lot of grief. Tyra also asked Kimora Lee Simmons, another top supermodel and close friend, to be a judge on the show. Simmons said she was initially skeptical of reality TV, but that she would "always do anything to help Tyra." J. Alexander, a black gay male runway instructor from the Bronx who had taught Tyra how to strike a pose, was also recruited to teach the contestants how to walk the runway. When Tyra's mother called him to see if he would consider the job, J. Alexander said he thought it was just going to be another job. "No one had any idea the show was going to get this big," he later said.[14]

The crew shot the show in a furious eight weeks, doing each episode on the cheap for about $500,000, or about half of what it costs today. Tyra outfitted the contestants in her own wardrobe, and Mok negotiated with Manhattan's Flatotel hotel to house the cast and crew in exchange for television promotion. The judging room was so tiny that the cast felt like they were in a sardine can. Tyra, who suffers from irritable bowel syndrome, recalls that the stress caused her to have an attack "every single day of production."[15]

FEAR OF SUCCESS IN BUSINESS

As far as she'd come, Tyra told *Entertainment Weekly* that she was still skeptical about her rising status. "There's a fear I have with success in the business world," she said. "People have this image of women, especially in business, that they have to be ballbusters, and that's so not what I am. I'm not afraid of wanting money at all. Money will give me more power to do things that are true to my spirit than what I'm already doing. I don't think I'll always be on television. I don't know whether it's 10 or 20 years, but I know it won't be when I'm 60."[16]

TYRA'S BAD HAIR DAYS

While many of Tyra's bad days in recent history, including bouts with the press, "fat" photographs, and TV reality shows that bombed, were plastered across the media, Tyra says it's a good thing the media wasn't around for the worst days of her life—or when she was an adolescent, a period of her life she says she would never want to repeat. As Tyra recounts in her tell-all book, *Tyra's Beauty Inside & Out*, she was a skinny, ugly, awkward, and geeky girl whom her classmates called a variety of nasty nicknames, including "Lightbulb Head." Tyra said she was about as close to looking like a supermodel as "Olive Oyl," another name her classmates called her.[17]

Like many young girls her age, Tyra always wanted what she didn't have. Although she was born with pretty, light, sandy, brown hair, at age 13 Tyra wasn't happy with it because she wanted to look like her best friend, Jamaillie, who had coal black hair that was super shiny. Without telling her mother, Tyra went to the hairdresser and told her that her mother had told her it was OK to dye it jet black. "Of course, that was a big fat lie," says Tyra in her book. "My mother was totally against my getting any permanent color until I was at least sixteen. But I thought I was so smart." Tyra took a big, floppy hat to the hair salon to wear home to cover up the dye job so her mother wouldn't notice it. Fat chance of that when Tyra decided she'd better keep the hat on through dinner, and even after dinner to do her homework.

Of course, this aroused her mother's suspicion. But instead of confronting her daughter at dinner, Carolyn played it cool and ignored her—until the next morning, when she was right at Tyra's bed when she woke up (without her hat on, of course!). Carolyn was so angry that Tyra had dyed her hair without her permission that she grounded Tyra for a month. "I may not have been able to leave the house for 30 days, but I still had my black hair, and that was all that mattered," Tyra recalls.[18]

LOOK, MA, NO HAIR!

Tyra's secret dye job was just the first of many insults she and others inflicted on her hair in the name of glamour and beauty. When she became a supermodel, her hair was continually subjected to the whims of hair stylists. In one day, her hair could be crimped, teased, hairsprayed flat, fried with a flattening iron, twisted into dreadlocks, waved and curled with curling irons—all without any washing or shampooing in between, she says in her book. The damage eventually took its toll, and one day, not long into her modeling career in Paris, Tyra noticed her hair was falling out in clumps. Tyra was forced to get a hair weave to hide the damage, and continues to wear one today, often reminding her talk show guests that those lovely locks aren't her own. "If you see any photos of me with my hair down to my butt, just know that it ain't my natural hair."[19]

"LIGHTBULB HEAD"

Tyra didn't just obsess about her hair when she was a young girl and a teen. She also obsessed about the shape and size of her body. When she was 11 years old, over a three-month period, she lost nearly 20 pounds and grew three inches. At 5´, 9´´ and 98 pounds, Tyra was so tall she towered over her classmates and even her teachers, and she was so thin her parents and teachers feared she had an eating disorder or terrible illness and took her to see several specialists. Although doctors said Tyra was perfectly healthy, her unusual body proportions made her stick out in all the wrong ways. Before her body had taken on its bizarre proportions, she had been popular in school and an extrovert. But when Mother Nature stepped in and turned her into a bean stalk, she became self-conscious, introverted, and shy, hiding behind books to avoid the rude stares of others.[20]

In an attempt to gain weight, Tyra binged on unhealthy junk food, stuffing herself with greasy fried foods, ice cream shakes, and artery-clogging goods. But nothing seemed to work. It wasn't until she turned 17 that she actually began gaining weight and developing curves. And talk about bad timing![21]

TOO FAT TO BE A SUPERMODEL

Tyra's weight gain came around the same time her modeling career took off. Now, instead of being too skinny, she was considered too fat! At age 18, Tyra wore a size 8 in an industry where the norm was a size 0 or 2. Because she was so fully endowed, she couldn't' work with a lot of designers because their clothing was tailored with a size 2 in mind. According to Tyra, the designers' attitude was that if you wanted to work with them, you had to be able to fit into their clothing—no if's, and's, or but's. Since Tyra was unable to magically shed pounds and reduce herself down several sizes, she lost out on a lot modeling gigs. In fact, at one time there was a long list of designers who refused to work with Tyra because of her measurements.[22]

In her book, Tyra said she was fortunate to have role models in the modeling business like Iman, Helena Christiansen, Claudia Schiffer, and Cindy Crawford who weren't Twiggy-thin. Looking at their success helped Tyra stop listening to the many people in the modeling industry who tried to make her feel insecure because of her larger size and helped her appreciate her voluptuous body for what it was. Tyra said the fan mail she received also helped her appreciate her shapely physique. "To someone on the street, I may look pretty slim, but in the modeling world, my curves are the exception, not the rule," says Tyra.

> People tell me they are pleased that I am not super skinny and that I've got some meat on my bones. Those thousands of positive letters helped me realize how important it is for women to be able to open up a magazine and see a variety of models with varying shapes and body sizes. I've spent a lot time worrying about my body type, tripping on insecurities and doubting myself. But I decided I'm not going to obsess over things I can't do anything about. When I look in the mirror, I see that I have curvy hips and full breasts and that they're really not going anywhere. But that's okay. They're where they were meant to be.[23]

TEENAGE ROLE MODEL

Tyra said because of her mother's support, as a young model she was able to resist the temptation to succumb to the pressure. Unlike many other young models, Tyra never starved herself to stay thin or developed an eating disorder, although they were all around her in the modeling and fashion industry.

In her book Tyra talks about the many models she met during her career who engaged in unhealthy eating and lifestyle practices in an effort to maintain super-thin figures. Tyra said one young model didn't want to have breasts or hips, so she binded them with gauze to give herself a flat-chested appearance, and starved herself until she fainted to maintain her thin figure. When Tyra asked her why she was hurting herself like this, she said the waif look was "in" and she would lose jobs if she didn't remain thin. Tyra met another model at a fashion show in Paris who had lost so much weight that she almost resembled a concentration camp victim. When Tyra told the girl she looked like she had lost a lot of weight and appeared sickly, the model beamed back and thanked her for the compliment![24]

Today, many women's magazines have applauded Tyra for her courage in fighting against the modeling industry's preconceived notions of beauty. She has proven to the world that you didn't have to be white, stick-thin, or blessed with long, straight blond hair to become a supermodel. You can also make it if you're a black woman with curves and wavy brown hair.

CONSTANT ALLY

Given the amount of private and public rejection Tyra has endured, she says it's nice to know there's someone she can always rely on to give her love, sympathy, and the straight scoop. That person is her mother, Carolyn London-Johnson, her former manager and the wind beneath Tyra's wings when she feels discouraged and rejected. Like any mother hen, Carolyn was initially nervous about letting her daughter go off to Paris to model. "I let Tyra go, but I was terrified. I didn't sleep. I cried. She cried. From the beginning, she knew I didn't want her to go. She had a choice of going to college or going over there, and I let her know the decision had to be hers and that I would support her however I could," Carolyn said.[25]

"I learned very quickly that the fashion industry is very fickle and that the models have very little control over their careers. They come and go, and only a handful transcends every trend. We wanted that control, so we hired a publicist to let the public know who Tyra really is and what she is about. We said let's direct this to John Q. Public."[26]

TYRA'S MAN PROBLEMS

But there are some things that even the most supportive mother couldn't help or fix, and that included Tyra's love life. Although Tyra had graced the covers of many men's magazines, including *Sports Illustrated*, *GQ*, and *Esquire*, and was idolized from afar by millions of men around the world, Tyra didn't have the same sort of luck with men in her private life. In her book, Tyra recounts a series of dating disasters with older men that left her heartbroken. "Lately it seems I constantly get the court jester. But I figured I'll eventually hit on royalty," she wrote. In fact, when her book came out in 1999, Tyra told her readers that while most people assumed every guy desperately wanted to date a model, it was her personal experience that many of them didn't, either because they felt threatened by her because she made more money than they did, or because she was so famous. Other men simply dated her because they wanted to be seen with arm candy, she said, while others were more interested in her money than in her.[27]

Some of Tyra's most publicized love affairs went nowhere or fizzled out fast, including her relationship with film director John Singleton, whom she dated from 1993 to 1995 while starring in one of his films, *Higher Learning*. Because she was dating him when she got the part, the media claimed Singleton had given her the part because she was his girlfriend and not because of any acting talent she might have.

After Tyra broke up with Singleton, she had a brief fling with Seal in 1996, but the relationship ended almost as soon as it began, leaving Seal with a broken heart. He eventually got over Tyra and married Tyra's friend and fellow supermodel Heidi Klum. But the breakup was so traumatic for Seal that it fueled the emotional inspiration behind his 1998 album, *Human Being*, including his heartfelt plea for forgiveness in his song, "When a Man is Wrong."[28]

Between 2002 and 2004, Tyra dated Chris Webber, a professional basketball player. Rumors flew that the two were engaged after they were seen strolling together on a beach in Maui and Tyra had a rock on her ring finger. But that relationship also hit the rocks when Tyra broke up with him in 2004.[29]

In 2005, Tyra was convinced she had finally found her soul mate in Italian entrepreneur and former basketball star Giancarlo Marcaccini. "I'm not living in fear that I'll never find love anymore. I want to get married. I want to have kids and Marcaccini definitely fits the bill as Mr. Perfect," she told her talk show audience, adding that her ideal man is "a guy who's my age, who has a good job, and can take me out." At the time, Marcaccini was a 33-year-old hunk two years Tyra's senior, who owned a successful ice cream business. But like Tyra's other romances, that one also fizzled.[30] Tyra also dated her old high school sweetheart Craig Taylor, a law student at Fordham University, dispelling the myth that only rock stars and athletes get the supermodels. The lesbian-themed magazine, *Girlfriends*, dogged Tyra with rumors that she was bisexual, pointing to her relationship with WNBA star Teresa Weatherspoon, the point guard for the New York Liberty. The speculation heated up when Tyra refused to discuss her sexual preference, and by her comment, "I'm here to tell you that there is life without a man."[31]

For the past few years, Tyra has been dating New York investment banker John Utendahl of Wall Street's Utendahl Capital Partners. Rumors flew that Tyra was moving her talk show from Los Angeles to New York to be closer to Utendahl, but Tyra insisted there was no truth in it. "I'm very insulted by that rumor," she told *Essence*. "I employ a lot of people; their livelihoods rest on my shows. The move to New York was a decision I made with my manager. It was not about a man."[32]

In fact, it was clear that no man was filling the void Tyra felt for family and friends left behind in Los Angeles. After moving the show to New York, Tyra told *Essence* that life felt empty. "I'd go to work and women would be crying in my arms on the talk show. But then I'd go home and put my key in my door and . . . nothing: no friends, no husband, no children. I feel so full when I'm at work but so empty when I come home. After the talk show started, and I had *Top Model* at the same time, it engulfed me so much that it dulled my maternal instinct."[33]

Tyra also told the magazine her workaholic life had left little time or energy for thinking about having kids. "After the talk show started, and I had *Top Model* at the same time, it engulfed me so much that it dulled my maternal instinct," she said. "I hope that when I get more of a handle on my life, it comes back."[34]

TYRA'S STALKER

Tyra suffered man problems of a different order when a too-avid-fan, Brady Green, 39, of Dublin, Georgia, began stalking her. Green was recently convicted of stalking, harassment, criminal trespass, and attempted aggravated harassment—but not before he had stalked Tyra from coast to coast—calling her offices, showing up at her TV studios, and sending her flowers. Police said he even threatened to cut a staffer's throat for not telling him where Banks was. When Green was arrested March 18, 2008, at a McDonald's restaurant near Tyra's Manhattan studio, he told officers they "had a thing together," police said.[35]

Green's lawyer defended his client as an "overzealous fan" during a court appearance on April 17, insisting he just wanted to appear on Tyra's talk show, and insinuating that Tyra had brought the stalking on herself. "Tyra presents herself as someone her fans can relate to" and invites those "inspired by her shows to reach out to her," he said. But Tyra didn't buy it, and neither did the judge.[36]

In April 2009, Tyra took the stand as the first witness for the prosecution and told the court she had to bolster her security team and feared for her own safety and the safety of her family and staff members as a result of Green's actions. After hearing closing arguments, Manhattan Criminal Court Judge James Burke concluded, "The behavior was hounding." While Green could have been sentenced to 90 days in jail, he received no jail time. Burke advised Green's lawyer, "Put Mr. Green in a location where he can thrive. And that location is not likely to be the city of New York."[37]

In June 2008, the Georgia man was sentenced to a year of probation and ordered to complete a treatment program designed specifically for stalkers. Green was also ordered to stay away from the former supermodel for the next two years under an order of protection. Judge Burke warned Green that he would face up to 90 days in jail if he disobeyed any of the court's orders.[38]

Tyra said the stalker's actions have made her feel "extremely vulnerable. I know I have fans, but I've never in my entire career had my staff act this way," she said, adding that Green had been far more aggressive than most fans in showing his devotion—and not in a good way.[39]

NOTES

1. Kiri Blakeley, "Tyra Banks on It," *Forbes* (July 2006), www.forbes.com/free_forbes/2006/0703/120.html (accessed June 30, 2009).

2. Ibid.

3. Tyra Banks, *Tyra's Beauty Inside & Out* (New York: Harper Collins, 1998), 167.

4. "Tyra Banks Biography—Grounded in Family Love, Entranced the Paris Runways, Spotted by Influential Director," http://biography.jrank.org/pages/2497/Banks-Tyra.html.

5. Carol Brennan and Sara Pendergast, *Tyra Banks Contemporary Black Biography* (New York: Gale Group, 2005), 43.

6. Jay Schulberg, *The Milk Mustache Book* (New York: Ballantine Books, 1998), 6.

7. Quoted by Pam Levin, *Tyra Banks* (Philadelphia: Chelsea House Publishers, 2000), 62.

8. Ibid., 75.

9. Ibid., 60.

10. Quoted by Blakeley, "Tyra Banks on It."

11. Quoted by Tim Stack, "America's Next Top Mogul," *Entertainment Weekly*, February 19, 2008, www.ew.com/ew/article/0,,20178169,00.html (acccessed June 30, 2009).

12. Ibid., 34.

13. Ibid., 35.

14. Ibid.

15. Ibid., 32.

16. Stack, "America's Next Top Mogul."

17. Banks, *Tyra's Beauty Inside & Out*, 72.

18. Ibid.

19. Ibid., 75.

20. Ibid.

21. Ibid., 84–85.

22. Ibid.

23. Amy Elisa Keith, "How Tyra Banks Lost 30 Pounds," *CNN.com*, November 4, 2009, www.cnn.com/2009/SHOWBIZ/TV/11/03/tyra.banks.weight.diet/index.html.

24. Quoted by Levin, *Tyra Banks*, 24–25.

25. Quoted by Lila Chase, *Totally Tyra: An Unauthorized Biography* (New York: Penguin Group, 2006), 170.

26. Ibid.

27. Banks, *Tyra's Beauty Inside & Out*, 93.

28. Chase, *Totally Tyra*, 87.

29. Ibid.

30. Tyra Banks page, www.abstracts.net/tyra-banks (accessed June 14, 2009).

31. Ibid.

32. Quoted by Jeannine Amber, "Standing in the Spotlight," *Essence*, February 2008: 132.

33. Ibid.

34. Ibid.

35. "Tyra Banks Takes Stand in Stalker Case," *People*, April 28, 2009, www.people.com/people/article/0,,20275548,00.html (accessed June 8, 2009).

36. Quoted by Samuel Maull, "Tyra Banks' Stalker Needs Counseling," *AP Online*, April 30, 2009, www.highbeam.com/doc/1A1-D97T0AQG4.html (accessed June 8, 2009).

37. Samuel Maull, "Ga. Man Sentenced in NYC for Stalking Tyra Banks," *AP Online*, June 19, 2009, www.highbeam.com/doc/1A1-D98TM24G0.html (accessed June 8, 2009).

38. Chris Homer, "Terrified, Tyra Banks Testifies against Alleged Stalker, Who Says He Never Meant to Scare Her," *Digitalspy*, April 29, 2009, www.digitalspy.com (accessed June 9. 2009).

39. Ibid.

Chapter 9

TYRA ENTERS THE
POLITICAL ARENA

With the presidential election heating up, Tyra decided to use her talk show as a forum for discussion and sent out invites to all the candidates asking them if they would come on her show. Several accepted and made *The Tyra Banks Show* one of the few television programs to conduct one-hour interviews with leading presidential candidates, including Senator Barack Obama, Senator Hillary Clinton, Governor Mike Huckabee, and Senator John Edwards.[1]

If some of these candidates had never appeared on a talk show like Tyra's, she was in the same boat. Although she had interviewed a wide range of people, this would be her first foray into politics. Whether or not she had the political insights and savvy to pull information out of the candidates remained to be seen, but as usual, Tyra was up for a new challenge, even if many in the media thought she was hopelessly out of her league.

Unlike Oprah, who had already endorsed Barack Obama without interviewing other candidates, Tyra said she wanted to talk to as many candidates as possible on her show before making a commitment to one candidate, pointing out that endorsements from celebrities were often thoughtless and cheap. "If you look at a lot of people in the field we're in," Tyra told the *National Enquirer*, "[celebrities] are constantly endorsing everything—from a new purse to a new hotel. This is just another thing [to endorse]."[2]

While Tyra respected Oprah's choice to back Obama's presidential campaign and understood the influence it would have on others—"I love Oprah using her power, because she has the influence to change what she feels is necessary"—she wanted to leave her show open to all candidates. "We want as many candidates as will come on," she said. "We want both sides of the political spectrum."[3]

TYRA INTERVIEWS OBAMA

In September 2008, Tyra invited Democratic presidential nominee Barack Obama on her talk show. For the interview, she substituted a demure demeanor for her normally fierce, "you go, girlfriend" one, and seemed to hand over the reigns to Obama by letting him run the interview—a first for Tyra! Then again, she was wading in unfamiliar waters.

Tyra had actually met Obama long before he ever appeared on her talk show. She first ran into him at Oprah Winfrey's Legends Ball in 2005, in what she described as an "embarrassing situation" but one which also reflected Obama's down-to-earth nature.

> My friend Kimora Lee Simmons and I were walking around the ball. We had on these big Cinderella dresses—hardly anyone wore white tie, but we both did—and then we see Senator Obama. He goes, "Hi, ladies," and I told him, "I want to congratulate you on that speech. It was gorgeous." At the time, there was just a hint of him running for president. But then Kimora starts talking crazy, just totally embarrassing me. She walks away, and I'm like, "Senator Obama, I have to apologize for my friend. She's almost like family, I've known her since I was 17 years old, and with family, you love them but sometimes you want to say that you're not related to them." And he said, "What are you talking about? You don't think that I could be down and talk crazy like that? You think politicians are all stiff and can't relate? Come on, girl."[4]

On her talk show, Obama steered the interview towards nonpolitical topics such as his interracial family. At one point, he even asked Tyra's advice for gift suggestions for Michelle. Meanwhile, Tyra also did some predictably goofy things on her show that you'd never see on *Hardball* or *Anderson Cooper*, such as having Obama look into a crystal ball, and at one point she even threatened to give him a makeover. About the only time she pitched a hardball question to Obama was when she asked if she could spend a night in the Lincoln room at the White House. Obama politely ignored her request, which she made several times. It wasn't until after Obama had actually won the nomination that Tyra switched into high political gear on her talk show. "When Barack won the nomination, I just started bawling," she told her audience. "I started calling all these people, and everybody was talking to me like I was crazy. They're like, 'Well, he hasn't won yet,' but I'm like, 'Yes, he has, because he's gotten this far.' "[5]

TYRA GETS DOWN WITH HILLARY

In January, 1998, Tyra invited Senator Hillary Clinton on her show in another "political" interview that also veered far from the current political arena. Hillary broke her silence on the pain and anguish she went through after learning about her husband's dalliance with White House intern Monica Lewinsky, exactly a decade after the incident was first reported. In a soul-baring interview, she candidly revealed to Tyra how she worked through the inner torment, but added that she "never doubted" her husband's love for her. "I never doubted Bill's love for me, ever," she said on the show. "But I had to decide what I ought to do. I think it is so important to be able to hear yourself at a moment when it is hard . . . there are so many times when you really have to listen to yourself."[6]

Hillary told Tyra she was left humiliated after it emerged her husband had cheated on her with Lewinsky. Bill initially swore under oath that he "did not have sexual relations" with Lewinsky—but later admitted that he had misled the American public. Asked by Tyra if she had been embarrassed by the affair, Hilary replied: "Sure, all of that. But I was just praying so hard and thinking so hard about what's right to do that I couldn't let anything else interfere with that. The momentary feelings—you're mad, you're really upset, you're disappointed—all of that goes through your mind. But I have found that you really shouldn't make decisions in the heat of those moments. You have to think about it," she said.[7]

Hilary said, as a result of the incident she's become something of a poster child for women who have been cheated on and gets a lot of letters from women in similar circumstances asking her what they should do. "I say you have to be true to yourself," Hillary told Tyra. "No one story is the same as any other story. I don't know your reality. I can't possibly substitute my judgment for yours, but what I can tell you is you must be true to yourself. You have to do what is right for you."[8]

The interview wasn't all one big sob story. In more lighthearted moments, when asked what reality TV program she would prefer to compete on, Hillary said, "I think it would have to be *Dancing with the Stars*, especially if I could have one of those really good partners. In my dreams I would be on *America's Next Top Model* but in reality I would have to choose my limited talents and of them dancing is better than singing. You do not want me to sing." Hillary was apparently making a reference to her off-key rendition of "The Star-Spangled Banner," which has made the rounds on You Tube.[9]

She even suggested a nationwide contest, "like a reality show," for a title for her husband, former President Bill Clinton, should she win the nomination and be elected the nation's first female president. "Here are some of the things that have been suggested, like 'First Mate,' " Hillary said. "His Scottish friends say 'First Laddy,' but we need ideas. I'll just keep calling him Bill." Asked whether she does any of a number of popular dances, including hip-hop, Hillary said she had heard of them and that they were "variations of what I did like 30, 40 years ago. Everything gets recycled and gets a different name," she said.[10]

TYRA ROCKS OUT WITH MIKE HUCKABEE

Republican presidential hopeful Mike Huckabee also accepted an invitation to talk to Tyra on her show on February 29. Like the other interviews, the talk started out on a light note. Instead of giving her a lesson on government, the former Arkansas governor gave Tyra some quick tips on playing the bass guitar. "I took guitar before . . . well for two months but I remember nothing," Tyra told him. "My fingers used to hurt really bad when I played guitar. I stopped because of it."[11]

The show had been taped just after Mitt Romney announced he'd suspended his campaign, and Huckabee joked that his appearance on Tyra's talk show had prompted the former Massachusetts governor to drop out. "He heard I was coming on the show, Tyra, and he said if he's on Tyra's show, this is done for me." As for Huckabee, "I'm so pumped about being here," he told Tyra.[12]

But the levity didn't last for long. Tyra, a gay rights advocate who has been honored by GLAAD on several occasions, used her show as an opportunity to feel out Huckabee, a Christian conservative and preacher, on issues concerning homosexuality and gay marriage. Asking him if he thought homosexuality was immoral, Huckabee danced around the answer, saying, "I think that we were created to have relationships with someone of the opposite gender, that how's we reproduce, that's how we live our lives. I've had people who are gay that worked on my staff. It's not like I'm some homophobe. If you ask me, Is it the normal pathway? I don't think so. But, you know, I respect that people have different views about that."[13]

When Tyra asked him if he wanted the gay vote, Huckabee said,

Sure, I want every vote. Seriously, I want to be president of everybody. And I can disagree with people over a choice they make in their life or over a lifestyle and still be their president and still say I want to keep you free, I want to keep your country safe, I want to make your taxes lower not higher. I want to solve some issues like the problems we have in education and rebuild our health care system, and I think whether a person is straight or gay, they want a president who is solving issues, not just pointing out differences among people.[14]

But Huckabee drew his line in the sand when Tyra asked him about gay marriage. "What if they say, 'I want to vote for you, Governor Huckabee, but I'm a gay man and I want to marry my man?' What do you say to that?" Tyra asked him. Huckabee said he felt that changing the definitions of institutions like marriage "is beyond saying if people want to live a life that's different than others, that's fine, but when you redefine basic institutions of marriage, government, whatever they may be, that's when we really should have a pretty thorough public discussion about it."[15]

TYRA GOES ONE ON ONE WITH JOHN EDWARDS

In what was perhaps her least publicized and controversial interview, Tyra also interviewed John Edwards in January, surprising the

Democratic presidential candidate with a meal from Wendy's as a nod to where he and his wife celebrated their first and subsequent anniversaries. Edwards was challenging a black man and a woman for the presidential nomination, and when asked by Tyra what it felt like to be a minority and a white male, Edwards said, "It feels like you have to fight for everything you get. We have a couple of candidates who are good candidates but they get an enormous amount of attention and publicity, and they've got enormous amounts of money. The result is I have to really work to be heard." Edwards said that when he is heard, "people understand I have this personal energy and passion for what it is I'm trying to do, whether it's health care, creating jobs, doing the things that need to be done for the country."[16]

TYRA CHANNELS MICHELLE

Meanwhile, Tyra also got a chance to make a political statement in an arena in which she was far more experienced—on the pages of the September 2008 issue of *Harper's Bazaar*, where she portrayed Michelle Obama by dressing like her and posing with a model who resembled Barack Obama. Already a huge fan of Michelle—on her talk show, Tyra had said, "Michelle, you're one hot mama!"—Tyra jumped at the chance, claiming it would enable her to portray a potential first lady who reminded her a lot of the country's second first lady, Abigail Adams, as portrayed on the HBO series, *John Adams*, by actress Laura Linney. "She [Abigail] stood up for women. She was able to speak her mind about women's issues with her man, and he actually, truly listened to her," she said.[17]

Michelle, she said, was in the same boat. "With Barack Obama, his becoming president is them becoming president because Michelle was there from the beginning. Without Michelle, he wouldn't be there." Having already met her, Tyra found her "so warm and so gracious. She's got that direct-eye-contact, truly-connecting thing. She's not a 'ha, ha, ha' type. And I love that she's tall." Tyra added that for women, navigating politics was often a tricky proposition, pointing to Hillary Clinton as an example, who admitted to Tyra on her show that she often felt afraid to say anything because every word she said was picked apart and analyzed by the press. "And it's the same for Michelle

Obama, especially with her and Barack being the first, you know, in so, so many ways," Tyra told *Harper's Bazaar*, claiming a first lady would need a multitude of qualities to appeal to the American public. She would need to smile, not take herself too seriously, be comfortable being photographed in a variety of moods—"from being fierce to being photographed eating fried chicken with grease on her fingers," and "to feel like every child in America is hers." Tyra said it would also be nice if the first lady knew how to do her own makeup, although her most important quality would be acting as the president's "rock and his boulder and his mountain, and she should be calling about 50 percent of the shots!"[18]

When asked by *Harper's* how she'd dress if she ever reached the highest office in the land, she said she would "dress the part" in a V-neck shirt and a two-inch heel. Even if the president were taller, she'd keep her heels low to avoid coming across as too sexy, she said. As for her hair, she'd forego a Jackie flip and probably go with a weave. And her Secret Service acronym? "KMFA: Kiss My Fat Ass!"[19]

Tyra also said she felt having a black president would give everyone in the country more hope. She described one of her talk shows that had tested racism in small children by showing them pictures of a black man in a suit and a white man in a suit and asking them which one could be president. Although the children represented many different races, including black, not one of them chose the black man. "What gives me tears is if Barack Obama wins, kids are going to say that a black man can be president, too," said Tyra. "I think it will give so many people—black, Latin, Asian, even white people that feel forgotten—it gives them hope. I did not think I would see it in my lifetime, and I'm only 34."[20]

TYRA MAKES AN ENDORSEMENT

In November 2008, after interviewing not only Barack Obama but also presidential hopefuls Hillary Clinton, John Edwards, and Mike Huckabee (candidates John McCain, Mitt Romney, and Sarah Palin declined Tyra's invitations to appear on the show), Tyra publicly endorsed Obama for president. In a public statement, Tyra said she'd been won over by Obama's campaign for change "because Americans are desperate for better leadership following eight years under President George W. Bush's rule. Throughout the campaign I have been inspired by Senator Barack Obama and his message of change, and I believe he will uplift Americans during these critical times. I will be voting for Obama because I feel America is not only ready for this change, we are in need of it.[21]

TYRA TALKS TO LEVI JOHNSTON

Given Tyra's well-publicized backing of Obama, it was no surprise when Republican presidential nominees John McCain and vice presidential candidate Sarah Palin politely declined Tyra's invitations to appear on the show. But when Tyra extended an invite to Levi Johnston, Bristol Palin's ex-boyfriend who fathered her illegitimate son, Tripp, born on December 27, 2008, he was more than eager to come on the show and spill the beans. (Sarah Palin announced her daughter's pregnancy on September 1, 2008, just days after Senator John McCain picked her to be his Republican vice presidential running mate.)[22]

When Tyra asked Levi how things were going with Bristol and his infant son, Levi, 19, told Tyra that he and Bristol, 18, didn't always get along. "Some days we can have regular conversations without fighting. Most of the times, I don't know what's wrong with her. She's in a pretty bad mood, she's short, she doesn't want me around, I don't think. She says that I can come see the baby and that kind of thing, but won't let me take him anywhere." Levi said that he and Bristol had broken off their engagement because neither one of them were mature enough to enter into a marriage.[23]

When Tyra asked Levi if Sarah Palin knew he was shacking up with her daughter in her home, Levi said Sarah Palin probably knew he and Bristol were having sex. "Moms are pretty smart," he said. Levi later appeared at the Republican National Convention with the Palins. Levi told Tyra he went to the convention at Bristol's request, but he wasn't thrilled to attend it. "I felt out of place," he said.[24]

Interestingly, when Tyra asked Levi who he'd vote for in 2012 if the choice were President Barack Obama or Sarah Palin, he said, "I still think I'm going to have to vote for Sarah Palin."[25]

As you might expect, the Palm family was hardly thrilled with Levi's appearance on national television and his chat with Tyra about their family secrets. In a prepared statement, Palin family spokeswoman Meghan Stapleton said Bristol Palin "was unaware Johnston would be appearing on *The Tyra Banks Show*. We're disappointed that Levi and his family, in a quest for fame, attention and fortune, are engaging in flat-out lies, gross exaggeration, and even distortion of their relationship," she said. According to Stapleton, "Bristol Palin isn't preventing anyone from seeing the baby," and that Johnston sees his son "whenever he wants; the family sees the baby whenever they want."[26]

If Levi's appearance on Tyra's talk show was a piece of the puzzle that eventually defeated his mother-in-law and her running mate, John McCain, it catapulted Levi into the media ionosphere. By June 2009, he was in Los Angeles hunting stardom as an aspiring actor and model. According to his new manager Tank Jones, an Anchorage private investigator, he was also getting closer to clinching a deal that would help him support the baby son he fathered with Bristol. "There's offers on the table for a little bit of everything—sitcom appearances, a reality show, some modeling," Jones told *People*. "We haven't signed anything, but there's offers," he said, adding that Levi's interest in a show business "represents one of the few viable careers open to him." A high-school dropout passionate about hunting and hockey, Levi "is going to go and take the test and finish school and enroll in some college courses," his manager said. "But it's not like he can go and get a normal job now. Because of all the publicity. The whole interviewing thing [with Tyra and Larry King], and red carpet and paparazzi—he still hasn't gotten comfortable with it, but what else does he have? Can he go work at McDonald's? . . . He wants to take care of his son financially."[27]

Later, when David Letterman made off-color jokes about the Palin family, Levi said Bristol's feelings—and those of her younger sister, Willow, 14—were his biggest concern. "I don't think [Letterman] was trying to be malicious. I just think the joke maybe went too far," said Levi. "I don't like to see anybody hurt, especially if it got to the girls and their feelings were hurt."[28]

POLITICS AND POP CULTURE

The Washington press core and TV pundits may have been skeptical that Tyra had the interviewing skills to do a presidential candidate justice, but the candidates seized on the invites as an opportunity to connect with Tyra's millions of voter-age women viewers in a way they might not be able to do on a more serious talk show or in newspaper interviews. "We make every effort to meet and talk to voters where they are, and that's not just targeting the evening newscasts," Obama spokesman Bill Burton told the *Washington Post*. "Barack Obama is one guy all the time, whether he's talking to Brian Williams or Tyra Banks."[29]

Phil Singer, a former spokesman for Hillary Clinton, agreed that chat shows were a key weapon in the communications arsenal. "Before each primary election day, we'd try to schedule her on as many of these shows as possible," he told the *Washington Post*. You'd try to get her on the *Letterman* show or *Access Hollywood*. It gave people a chance to see a different side of her. We were at a financial disadvantage, and these shows command huge audiences."[30]

The *Hartford Courant* theorized that politicians were probably safer appearing on taped talk shows than in front of a live audience because they could rehearse the show beforehand—insults, jokes, and all—to make sure they set the right tone. "Lest there be any illusions about spontaneity, the candidates actually prepare for the satirical and entertainment shows," the *Hartford Courant* pointed out. One argument for melding politics and entertainment is that voters like it. They have an opportunity to measure their candidates on such factors as sense of humor, self-deprecation, and the ability to respond quickly. Truth be told, we expect our political leaders to have skill sets similar to that of entertainers."[31]

Which may explain why some prominent politicians—the late president Ronald Reagan, for instance, and California governor Arnold Schwarzenegger, "are able to make relatively effortless moves into government," explains Robert Thompson, a professor at Syracuse University. "Whatever else we say, a president is in fact the star of a four-year-long television series," he told the *Hartford Courant*. "Our democratic cousins abroad might look down on America's big appetite for pop-culture politics, but they haven't blazed new trails by pursuing politics as if it were an academic subject, either. Let's face it, politics and showbiz have developed a symbiotic relationship. They combine to whet our appetite for illusions, fantasy and, yes, happy endings. It's the eternal optimist thing."[32]

NOTES

1. "Tyra Won't Take Political Sides," *National Enquirer*, September 7, 2007, www.nationalenquirer.com/tyra_banks_politics _president/celebrity/64190 (accessed July 7, 2009).

2. Ibid.

3. Ibid.

4. "President Barack Obama/The Tyra Banks Show," *Tyra.com*, January 20, 2009, http://tyrashow.warnerbros.com/2009/01/word_of _the_day_change.php.

5. Laura Brown, "American Dream," *Harper's Bazaar*, September 2008, www.harpersbazaar.com/magazine/cover/tyra-banks-interview-0908?click=main_sr (accessed July 16, 2009).

6. Ibid.

7. Anna Dimond, "Hillary Clinton Talks Adultery with Tyra," *TV Guide*, January 15, 2008, www.tvguide.com/news/Hillary-Clinton-Talks-13153.aspx (accessed July 20, 2009).

8. Sarah Wheaton., "The Hillary-Tyra Show," *New York Times*, January 16, 2008, http://thecaucus.blogs.nytimes.com/2008/01/16/ the-hillary-tyra-show/?scp=3&sq=Dancing,%20Singing%20or% 20Modeling?%20Hillary%20Clinton%20Says%20She&st=cse (accessed July 21, 2009).

9. "Dancing, Singing or Modeling? Hillary Clinton Says She'd Work the Dance Floor," *AP Worldstream*, January 15, 2008, www .highbeam.com/doc/1A1-D8U645Q80.html (accessed July 15, 2009).

10. Ibid.

11. "Tyra Rocks Out with Mike Huckabee," *People*, February 8, 2008, www.people.com/people/article/0,,20177100,00.html (accessed July 21, 2009).

12. Ibid.

13. Ibid.

14. Ibid.

15. Ibid.

16. Brian Stelter, "John Edwards, Funny Guy," *New York Times*, January 23, 2008, http://thecaucus.blogs.nytimes.com/2008/01/23/john-edwards-funny-guy.

17. Brown, "American Dream."

18. Ibid.

19. Ibid.

20. Ibid.

21. "Banks Lends Backing to Obama Campaign," *WENN News*, November 2, 2008, www.wenn.com (accessed July 10, 2009).

22. Associated Press, "Bristol Palin's Ex Says They Don't Get Along," *Charleston Daily Mail*, April 6, 2009.

23. Ibid.

24. Ibid.

25. Ibid.

26. Ibid.

27. Sandra Sobieraj and Champ Clark, "Levi Johnston Hunts Stardom in Los Angeles," *People*, June 18, 2009, www.people.com/people/article/0,,20285906,00.html (accessed July 28, 2009).

28. Ibid.

29. Howard Kurtz, "Obama's Talk Show Advantage Is No Idle Chatter," *Washington Post*, November 3, 2008, www.washingtonpost.com/wp-dyn/content/article/2008/11/02/AR2008110202326.html (accessed July 22, 2009).

30. Ibid.

31. MCT News Service, "Partisan Politics Pervade Pop Culture World," *Hartford Courant*, October 21, 2008, www.courant.com/features/sns-200910210807mctnewsservbc-poppolitics-1stperso,0,4947714.story.

32. Ibid.

Chapter 10

DIVA OR DREAMGIRL? THE CONTROVERSY CONTINUES

Tyra Banks is world famous for her outer beauty. Her face has graced the covers of hundreds of magazines and appeared in hundreds of others, and she has also been in many television commercials, television shows, videos, and films. By 1997, Tyra had created an incredible black-model presence, following in the footsteps of Iman, the elegant black model from East Africa who was considered the first black supermodel.[1] In 1996, at age 22, Tyra was also the youngest black woman to be named to *Ebony*'s "15 Most Beautiful Black Women," an honor she shared with Oprah, Lena Horne, Jada Pinckett, and Vanessa Williams.[2]

And by the time she was 24, Tyra's beautiful image had already earned her millions of dollars. Tyra was only the third African American woman to appear on the cover of the *Sports Illustrated* Swimsuit Issue, and the first black model to grace the cover of GQ magazine and the Victoria's Secret catalogue. Many national magazines over the years have named Tyra to their annual lists of "Most Beautiful People," "Most Influential People," "Hardest Working Celebrities," and "Sexiest Women." Tyra was also named to *Time* magazine's list of "People Who Shape Our World." In 2008, *Fortune Magazine* ranked her at the top of its list of female entertainers for earning power, estimating her annual income at $23 million.

STRAIGHT FROM THE HEART

But Tyra has always maintained—and demonstrated—that she has never sought out fame and fortune for its own sake. From the very beginning of her successful career as a model, she has used her fortune to help others, in particular, young disadvantaged teenage girls. Unlike many celebrities who merely lend their name to a cause, Tyra has been an active participant in every program she has sponsored, preferring "one-on-one" contact. "Many times celebrities just lend their names to a pet project, but I like one-on-one contact. Just seeing a smile on a child's face brightens my day," she wrote in her book, *Tyra's Beauty Inside & Out*.[3]

And Tyra didn't wait until she was a mega-millionaire to begin helping others. She started volunteering at the very start of her career. When she returned from Paris in 1992, she used some of her earnings to establish a scholarship fund for teenage girls at her alma mater, Immaculate Heart High School in Los Angeles. Tyra has also encouraged other young women to help others, not just for the good it would do others, but for the good it would do them. As she told the teenage girls at the first awards luncheon for the Tyra Banks Scholarship, "It's really just beautiful and wonderful, you know, to really help people, but it also makes you feel good about yourself, and I really believe in strong self-esteem, especially with young women."[4]

In keeping with what she called her passion to help children, Tyra also became a spokeswoman for The Center for Children & Families in New York City, an organization that helps abused and neglected children. Tyra also sponsored the center's Kidshare toy drive, in which children could experience the joy of giving a gift to someone else. Since the children could not afford to buy gifts themselves, Tyra campaigned for gifts from corporations and the public. For her dedication to the children, in 1997 Tyra was awarded The Friendship Award by the Starlight Children's Foundation of California.[5]

In 1999, Tyra and her mother, Carolyn, established TZone, a leadership camp for disadvantaged teenage girls from four high schools in the Los Angeles area. She became an active participant, spending her summers at the camp to be with campers every step of the way and serve as a friend, mentor, and big sister. Tyra chose every activity, down to each and every day's menu. Although the campers were initially intimidated by Tyra—the first day, they asked her for her autograph—by the end of camp they felt so comfortable with her they were calling her by her camp nickname, "BBQ."[6]

HELPING OTHERS HIT THE RUNWAY

Even Tyra's entrance into the entertainment world was partially motivated by her desire to help other women reach their goals. After a two-year stint as youth correspondent for Oprah, Tyra wanted to create a show where people were striving for a goal, winning something they worked hard for. "Tyra was constantly barraged by people asking her how she had made it in the modeling world." As she joked to the *Washington Post*, "There are so many people coming up to me and asking how to get into the modeling business. I thought, 'How can I get all these people off my back?' "[7]

The result was *America's Next Top Model*, which premiered in the spring of 2003. For the first season, 10 girls (the number expanded to 12, then 14, in later seasons) moved into a fabulous residence together (one year, it was a Manhattan penthouse in New York's historic Waldorf-Astoria hotel) and endured a sort of model boot camp as the camera followed them around, with the weakest contestant being eliminated at the end of each episode. The judges in the first season included former supermodel Janice Dickinson, whose caustic and blunt comments to the girls often left them in tears and caused the media to cast Dickinson as a "meanie." In season five, Tyra finally replaced her with supermodel Twiggy, who she chose to judge not only because she was a nice person, but because Tyra thought she could be a mother figure to the girls. To this day, Tyra has not only demanded that the judges treat the girls with respect, but also that the girls threat themselves with respect.[8]

Tyra also used her modeling show to change things she believed were wrong with the modeling industry, including contestants who represented the country's wide spectrum of colors, races, shapes, and sizes. "Who is going to connect with ten skinny blondes on TV? I wanted women of all colors, ranging from skinny to full-bodied—the idea was for women to see reflections of themselves."[9]

EMPOWERING THE DREAMS OF YOUNG WOMEN

In 2005, with *America's Next Top Model* going strong, Tyra finally got the chance to fulfill her life's s dream of hosting her own talk show for women, telling the *Miami Times* she wanted a show that would focus on "the dreams, hopes and challenges of today's young women, with a goal of empowering women to be the best they can be for themselves, their families and their communities."[10] Tyra introduced the first runway to daytime TV as a place for women "to strut and be proud when they needed an instant injection of self-confidence." Tyra said she hoped her talk show would provide young women "with the building blocks and an action plan they need to make their lives better." Claiming Tyra was "already a role model for young women everywhere," the *Miami Times* praised Tyra for "bringing her message of inner-beauty and self-confidence as the keys to success to a broader audience with her new talk show."[11]

IS THERE ANYTHING TYRA CAN'T DO?

Like *America's Next Top Model*, *The Tyra Banks Show* also exceeded all expectations, quickly becoming the top-ranking show in its time slot for women between the ages of 18 and 35. By the time Tyra was 34, some women's magazines were wondering if there was anything Tyra couldn't accomplish.

"From the runway to the oval office, everything is possible for Tyra Banks," wrote *Harper's Bazaar* in September 2008, pointing out that during Tyra's 20-year career, she had been a "first" in many ways, from being appointed a supermodel, a "hero and pioneer," to becoming "the new Oprah."[12]

The *New York Times Magazine* also recently threw in a comparison to Martha Stewart. "Banks has traded in her pretty for something far more compelling," wrote *Harpers Bazaar*, "a voice in the culture (especially to young women; some of the Tyra show's 1.5 million viewers are as young as 12) that is growing in influence every year. Her inclusive, enthusiastic promotion of self-esteem, positive body image, confidence, and beauty—even frank discussions on female anatomy, with a puppet—has struck a chord with women, while her 'You go, girl!' persona has won her something of a camp following as well."[13]

TYRA'S FINEST MOMENT

Nearly everyone in the media would agree that Tyra's finest moment occurred in 2007, when a blurry, unflattering photograph of her in a one-piece was splashed all over international tabloids and the Web, along with headlines so vicious—"Tyra Porkchop" and "America's Next Top Waddle." Even the most secure woman would have run to the nearest diet doc or plastic surgeon. But not Tyra. As embarrassed as she was by the photos, she decided the best strategy was to speak out, not run and hide. She went on her talk show in the same bathing suit and admitted she had gained 30 pounds since she was on the cover of *Sports Illustrated* a decade ago. Then she called for all women to accept themselves as they are, creating the famous "So What!" campaign.[14]

MORE THAN A BODY

It was all part of Tyra's long-running battle with the fashion and modeling industries to lay off the American women and stop feeding them unrealistic and unattainable notions of what was beautiful—a challenge Tyra personally faced from the time she was a voluptuous supermodel who couldn't fit into some of the designers' size 0 clothing. As she told the *New York Times* in 2005, "You know what, I've got dimples in my booty, and that's just the way it is. What separates me from other models is that it's not just about my body. If it was, then I wouldn't work. It's the personality, being able to sell the product and relate to the customer that makes up for other things that aren't perfect."[15]

In fact, Tyra relished having her own weight put in the spotlight, claiming it gave her the chance to address the issue from a personal view, in a way she never could before. "I was raised by women who don't believe that being super-skinny is the epitome of beauty," she told *Shape* magazine. "Being the best that you can be? That's beautiful, and I wanted to find a way to encourage every woman to love her body."[16]

TYRA'S TAKE ON HEALTH AND FITNESS

Tyra also used her embarrassing exposure in the press as a platform for emphasizing the importance of eating and exercising for health, admitting she didn't always take her own advice. During her modeling days, Tyra said she stayed thin because she often didn't have to eat well. "Sometimes the only thing in my kitchen when I got home at night was Tang and microwave popcorn, so that was my dinner," she told *Shape*.[17] Tyra said while she was heavier than she had been in her modeling days, she was also a lot healthier, and planned to stay that way by sticking to a diet of fresh fruits (her favorites are mangos and papayas) and salads with chicken, shrimp, or other protein. Tyra said she had even hired a part-time chef to cook meals for her so she had them at night. "I realized I needed to take better care of myself, and I knew this would be the best way to do that," she told *Shape*.[18]

When it comes to getting regular exercise, Tyra's doctor told her it wasn't an option but a necessity, writing her a prescription stating that she should do an hour of cardiovascular exercise every day. As a result, Tyra said she's been much more diligent about staying in shape. "Hey I'm only human," she told *Shape*. "When I see someone running around without any cellulite, I think, 'Gosh, I wish my butt could be that smooth.' But doing what I can to take care of myself means I don't worry about that so much."[19]

TYRA PROVES THERE IS LIFE AFTER MODELING

Tyra has also showed the world that there's life after modeling. "I think I showed the girls that it doesn't have to be over," Tyra told *Harper's Bazaar*. "They don't have to marry a rich man and trade in their pretty." Tyra recalled to the magazine that after retiring from modeling in 2005, she had a conversation with a famous supermodel to ensure she had a plan for what she was going to do after she stopped modeling. The supermodel looked at Tyra as if she had slapped her in the face and told her she would always model. But Tyra gave her some wise counsel, suggesting she think of herself as an athlete and realize that a day will come when she can no longer be a supermodel, or even a model.[20]

JUST AN ORDINARY LADY

Despite her fame and fortune, Tyra told *Ebony* in 2008 that she has the same money concerns as women who don't make millions have. She told the magazine she was decorating a new apartment in New

York and that when she met with the designer, she planned to tell him, "I don't care how much money they say I make in a year. It could be more, it could be less. But you don't need to be looking at that number and spending my money as if it is yours."[21]

Tyra also told Ebony she preferred shopping and dining at economical places, such as Crate & Barrel and The Cheesecake Factory. She also told the magazine she enjoyed showing off her imperfections— whether it was on her talk show or in her book. By being candid, and by creating a Tyra-world where beauty was within everyone's reach, Tyra said she hoped to force a change in America's view of what's pretty and what's not.[22]

Tyra added that while she's received many offers to put her name on products, including Tyra perfumes, Tyra lipsticks, Tyra pillows, and Tyra comforters, to date she has refused them all. "I don't just want to throw my name on stuff like that," she told Ebony. "Oh, my God, I've had the opportunity. And I could have retired off of doing that type of stuff. I just feel that the marketplace for celebrities throwing their names on things is oversaturated."[23]

AN ORDINARY FRIEND AND BOSS

People who have known Tyra personally and professionally would agree she's no diva. Tyra's best friend Kenya Barris, who met Tyra in kindergarten (they were seated alphabetically) and who later helped her bring America's Next Top Model to production, told Ebony that Tyra had always worked hard and saved her money, regardless of how much she was earning. "Tyra was making $70,000 to $80,000 a year modeling while in high school, but she refused to buy an 'it' car," he said. "Any one of us would have gotten a Cherokee, but she kept that Nissan Sentra well into our college years. She drove it literally until the wheels fell oft: The thing she is impressed with is getting a deal on something. She gets a kick out of being frugal."[24]

NO PRIMA DONNA AT WORK

Ken Mok, the executive producer for America's Next Top Model and Stylista, told the New York Times that Tyra is anything but a prima donna at work. While Mok admitted he was prepared for Tyra to be a producer of the series in name only, he was pleasantly surprised to find there was nothing too lowly for her to tackle. "She's not only appearing in front of the camera, but she's on set prepping the girls, styling them, putting on their makeup. It's an amazing thing to see. She's an incredibly ambitious woman who has a very, very good big-picture view, and she's also very much in control without acting like a control freak," he said. "She has a clear and distinct vision of her future as she shifted her role from being in front of the camera to behind it."[25]

Mok, who has worked with Tyra for six years, categorized her as the type of child, who, when growing up, was more interested in owning the candy store than working at it. "With the smarts that she has, and the hard work ethic that she has, it's no surprise that Tyra has achieved such fame and fortune," he told the *New York Times*.[26]

John Redmann, executive producer of *The Tyra Banks Show* who has worked with her for five seasons, told the *New York Times*, "You don't have to kiss her ass and tell her, 'Oh, my God, you are so amazing.' You can talk to her like a producer. There's no intimidation factor with her on that level. She values other people's opinions."[27]

WOULD RATHER DATE NON-CELEBS

Unlike many celebrities, Tyra also prefers to keep things low-key when it comes to whom she dates, preferring to go out with men who aren't celebrities and to stay out of the limelight when she's out and about. When *Ebony* asked Tyra how she meets men, she said she did it the way other women did. "It's the hookup!" she said. "One thing I can say is I try not to date people who are famous because one celebrity plus another celebrity equals five. The paparazzi will just start mixing my name with theirs. I find it fascinating looking at other celebs dating each other and I'm like, 'Look how cool they look!' But it's not a personal interest of mine. I get set up by friends." Tyra has most recently been connected to New York banker John Utendahl, who was certainly no household name before he hooked up with Tyra.

TYRA'S DETRACTORS

No biography of Tyra would be honest or balanced without a word from her critics. And despite the kudos piled on Tyra, she's been slammed by TV critics on many levels, but especially for her role as talk show host. According to the *New York Times*, while it "seemed fitting that Tyra would be the one to take the world of modeling to the mass audience [because] in some ways she seems to have more in common with her show's striving contestants than her established peers, a down-home quality that suggests she'd rather spend an evening at Applebee's than at Davé in Paris," her efforts to become the next Oprah were not nearly as successful.[28]

According to the *Times*, "Tyra [has been] less successful in her role as talk show host as she fumbled through a wildly discordant mix of stunts and self-help in yet another seedy showcase of afternoon depravity, one that gawks at the various dysfunctions it purports to remedy."[29]

The *Times* also lashed out at Tyra's interviewing style as well as her sincerity and talent, claiming her talk shows were often an example of "mentoring turns into hectoring. Couples arrive on her couch to discuss infidelity or abandonment, and she plays the concerned therapist for a few minutes. She teases out information until she arrives at some salacious episode that causes her to rumple her pretty face as if she were suddenly scandalized. Then she issues some simplistic advice meant to help the sad subject whom she has just exposed as a loveless geek or cheating tramp."[30]

TYRA THE HYPOCRITE

But the *Times* was most critical of Tyra for posing as virtuous and wholesome, then turning around and using her show to exploit a variety of sleazy sexual issues for ratings. The newspaper said Tyra had set "a tawdry tone" when she decided to resolve "the supposedly burning question" of whether her breasts were enhanced with implants. In "a desperate gambit for attention, she invited an expert to examine her on her show to test their authenticity. Such a ploy is strange for a woman who usually preaches the virtues of dignity, creativity and can't-touch-this fierceness." In another instance, Tyra used her talk show to discuss "tryyyy-sexuals," or couples who would try anything to reenergize their sex life," said the *Times*, calling it "a pathetic attempt to improve ratings. Tyra, the untouchable goddess, has not only come down to earth, but now she's luring us into some sex dungeon. There are much better places she could have taken us."[31]

TYRA'S NO DOWN-HOME GIRL

In fact, according to the *New York Times*, Tyra was a poseur who was far from the down-home, ordinary "girlfriend" she pretended to be on her reality shows and in the media. "Sure, she can make confessions about her ample rump or her forehead that is so high that people call her 'Fivehead,' but no one forgets for a minute that she belongs to an elite group of idealized females who make vulnerable people feel that much more uncomfortable," wrote the *Times*. "These gazelles are Ms. Banks's crowd, and when she is away from her *Top Model* coterie, she looks out of place, towering over stubbier figures. It's admirable that she thinks her skills at encouraging personal growth can fit a larger audience, but she's never quite at one with them, no matter how hard she tries to pitch hurricane-relief efforts or support-the-troops segments."[32]

MY, WHAT PRETTY CLAWS

The media was also critical of Tyra's choice of judges on *America's Next Top Model*, claiming she had hired tyrants who proceeded to inflict a series of horrors on the contestants. "Tears are shed and claws are bared, but few contestants are nastier than Janice Dickinson, one of the on-camera judges," reported the *New York Times*. "A former top model, Ms. Dickinson, author of *Everything About Me Is Fake . . . And I'm Perfect*, delights in delivering withering Simon Cowellesque assessments. 'If a girl is too short or too fat, or she is slovenly and hobbles in front of me, or if she looks like the closest she's ever gotten to a photographer is the one at the D.M.V., I'm going to say something.'"[33]

Off air, Dickinson was no less tolerant of contestants—or even Tyra. "I think the girls have been average so far," she said, then twisted the knife by claiming that working with Tyra had been "arduous," and that she, not Tyra, was the real star of the show. "I don't agree with the concepts or the choices," she told the *New York Times*. Although Tyra could not be reached for comment, UPN covered Dickinson's butt by claiming she was always one to "stir the pot" and "say anything for a reaction. That's why Tyra hired her and why she's an interesting judge. But it's a good thing she isn't a TV critic." Tyra finally got tired of Janice's antics, and booted her off the show, but it hardly put an end to their bickering.

In 2008, after being fired from the show, Janice accused Tyra of wrongly using her book, *No Lifeguard on Duty*, to give young girls advice on sex and drug use and then taking credit for it. "I mean, the thing looks so worn it's like she's been reading it on the toilet," said Janice. "It's pathetic. Where's her originality? Does she have no shame?"[34]

AMERICA'S NEXT TOP MODEL IS A HOAX!

Unfortunately, Janice Dickinson wasn't the only former judge who turned on Tyra after being fired from the show. Adrianne Curry, the winner of the first season of *America's Next Top Model*, lashed out at Tyra, who made her famous, in the February 2006 issue of *Playboy*. At 5′ 10′′, the green-eyed woman worked as a waitress before winning the competition and had a unique drive, gaining the respect of many judges when she showed up to elimination while battling food poisoning. After winning the title, Curry claimed she had gotten her modeling career going without the help of Tyra, and that without Tyra's help, she had been paid $1 million to pose nude for the magazine, making her the first contestant on the show to pose for the magazine.[35]

"She's really mean. She's Dr. Jekyll, Mr. Hyde," Curry told the *New York Post*, claiming that neither Tyra nor the show's producers had honored their promises to contestants when the show ended.

> She can be the sweetest person in the world, but once that camera is off, she's Naomi Campbell, in your face. Tyra really didn't help us out and the show didn't put any money into us . . . I was supposed to get a Revlon contract, but that fell through. We trusted Tyra but we've all been screwed over. There were a lot of things told to us that didn't show up on camera. Like, telling us if you win you're going to be a millionaire— It's called reality TV manipulation. Now that I'm a vet I understand, but when you're some lowly waitress from Joliet, Illinois, and Hollywood is filling your head with promises of scripts and gold, you buy into it pretty quickly.[36]

WINNERS GO NOWHERE

One could have accused Curry of sour grapes had not the venerable *New York Times* concurred with her accusations that *America's Next Top Model* had given contestants false hopes. When the *Times* pointed out that few, if any, of the winners had actually made it big in modeling, people began wondering if Tyra's detractors were right about her. "Just as few of the couples on romance-driven reality series like *The Bachelor* live happily ever after, few of the girls from *America's Next Top Model* have gone on to modeling careers of any renown," wrote the *Times*.[37]

Amy Astley, editor of *Teen Vogue*, also agreed the show was pushing the limits. "I'm not convinced the show's contestants can compete in the big leagues with first-name-only girls like Liya, Natalia and Gisele, or land in the glossy pages of major fashion magazines," she told the *Times*. "I think most professionals would look at these girls and say they're pretty, but not only do they not have what it takes to be a top model, they don't have what it takes to be a working model. It's a good reality soap opera and it's impressive that Tyra's leveraging her fame and expertise, but I think it's doing a bit of disservice to the modeling and fashion industry."[38]

TYRA KEEPS PUSHING

Despite the mounting criticism of Tyra and her reality TV shows, her fortune continues to skyrocket. In 2009, *Forbes* ranked her number 12 on the list of top female performers, claiming that between June 2008 and June 2009 she had earned an estimated $30 million—$8 million more than the previous year.[39]

Meanwhile, a number of publications, including *Newsweek*, the *New York Times Magazine*, and *Entertainment Weekly* have christened Tyra a "mogul," lumping her in the same venerable category as Oprah and Martha, much to Tyra's protests. "Don't get me wrong. Ego-wise, when I see the cover of the magazines and they say that I'm a mogul, I'm like 'oh, that looks popping and it looks hot, but it ain't true,'" Tyra told *Ebony*. "Oprah's been doing this for 30 years. Mogul? That's like Martha Stewart. That's like going public. Mogul? Not yet. But I have really big aspirations," admitted Tyra, claiming her stylist often asked her, "When will it be enough?"[40]

When *Ebony* asked Tyra the same question, she said she wouldn't stop until she had achieved the likes of Oprah and Martha—a feat she estimated would take her about ten years. Said Tyra, "I think I'll have an empire."[41]

NOTES

1. Joy Bennett Kinnon, "The 15 Most Beautiful Black Women," *Ebony*, October 1, 1996, www.highbeam.com/doc/1G1-18736500.html (accessed July 28, 2009).

2. Lila Chase, *Totally Tyra: An Unauthorized Biography* (New York: Penguin Group, 2006), 184.

3. Tyra Banks, *Tyra's Beauty Inside & Out* (New York: Harper Collins, 1998), 184.

4. Pam Levin, *Tyra Banks* (Philadelphia: Chelsea House Publishers, 2000), 4.

5. Chase, *Totally Tyra*, 55–57.

6. Quoted by Chase, *Totally Tyra*, 83.

7. Chase, *Totally Tyra*, 66–67.

8. Ibid., 68.

9. "Tyra Banks to Host Her Own Talk Show," *Miami Times*, September 13, 2005, www.highbeam.com/doc/1P1-117231755.html (accessed July 22, 2009).

10. Ibid.

11. Ibid.

12. Laura Brown, "American Dream," *Harper's Bazaar*, September 2008, www.harpersbazaar.com/magazine/cover/tyra-banks-interview-0908 (accessed July 21, 2009).

13. Ibid.

14. Claire Connor, "Why I Love My Body . . . Just the Way It Is," *Shape*, June 1, 2007, www.shape.com (accessed July 23, 2009).

15. Lola Ogunnaike, "My, What Pretty Claws," *New York Times*, September 26, 2004, www.nytimes.com/2004/09/26/fashion/26 TYRA.html?_r=1.

16. Connor, "Why I Love My Body."

17. Ibid.

18. Ibid.

19. Ibid.

20. Brown, "American Dream."

21. Adrienne P. Samuels, "Tyra Unexpected: Smart But Not Cheap, Tyra Banks Swears She's Just and Ordinary Lady," *Ebony*, December 1, 2008, www.highbeam.com/doc/1G1-189551743.html (accessed July 24, 2009).

22. Ibid.

23. Ibid.

24. Ibid.

25. Ogunnaike, "My, What Pretty Claws."

26. Ibid.

27. Ibid.

28. Ned Martel, "For the Most Part, Far from the Modeling Crowd," *New York Times*, November 2, 2005, www.nytimes.com/ 2005/11/02/arts/television/02mart.html?_r=1 (accessed July 24, 2009).

29. Ibid.

30. Ibid.

31. Ibid.

32. Ibid.

33. Ogunnaike, "My, What Pretty Claws."

34. "Dickinson Attacks Rival Banks," *WENN News*, May 19, 2008, www.imdb.com/news/ni0183381 (accessed July 25, 2009).

35. Adrianne Curry profile, *Playboy*, February 2006, www.playboy .com (accessed July 27, 2009).

36. "Page Six," *New York Post*, February 20, 2005, www.nypost .com (accessed July 24, 2009).

37. Martel, "For the Most Part, Far from the Modeling Crowd."

38. Ibid.

39. Lacey Rose, "Hollywood's War of the Wages," *Forbes*, July 2009, www.forbes.com/2009/06/11/jolie-aniston-limbaugh-stern-business-media-star-rivals.html (accessed August 4, 2009).

40. Samuels, "Tyra Unexpected."

41. Ibid.

Appendix A

PRODUCTIONS AND APPEARANCES

Executive Producer/Producer

1998
Honey Thunder Dunk (television movie)

2003–2009
America's Next Top Model (television series)

2004
Marple: The Body in the Library (television movie)

2005–2009
The Tyra Banks Show (television series)

2008
Stylista (television series)

2008
The Clique (Direct-to-DVD)

2008
Australia's Next Top Model (one episode)

2008
Are You Model Material?

2009
True Beauty (television series)

Films/Television Appearances

1992
Inferno, directed by Ellen Von Unwerth

1993
The Fresh Prince of Bel Air (7 episodes), directed by Shelley Jensen

1995
Higher Learning, directed by John Singleton

1997
New York Undercover (3 episodes), created by Kevin Arkadie and
   Dick Wolf

1998
Elmopalooza!, directed by Ann Marie Kearns

1999
Love Stinks, directed by Jeff Franklin

1999
The Hughleys (1 episode), produced by D. H. Hughley

1999
Felicity (3 episodes), *directed by* Tyrone S Walker.

1999
The Apartment Complex, directed by Tobe Hooper

2000
Coyote Ugly, directed by David McNally

2000
Life-Size, directed by Mark Rosman

2000
Love & Basketball, directed by David McNally

2000
MADtv (2 episodes), directed by Bruce Leddy

2000
O Brother, Where Art Thou, directed by Chris Weitz

2001
Soul Food (1 episode), directed by George Tillman, Jr.

2002
Eight Crazy Nights (voice), directed by Seth Kearsley

2002
Halloween: Resurrection, directed by Rick Rosenthal

2002
Fashiontrance, directed by Kira Wagner

2002
Larceny, directed by Irving Schwartz

2002
Cleavage, directed by Russ Meyer

2008
Tropic Thunder, directed by Ben Stiller

2008
All of Us, directed by Emily Abt

2009
Hannah Montana: The Movie, directed by Peter Chelsom

Soundtrack

2000
Life-Size, performs "Be a Star"

Single

2002
"Shake Ya Body"

Biographical Movie

2005
E! True Hollywood Story: Tyra Banks

Portrayed in

1975
Saturday Night Live

Magazine Covers

September 1990
Marie Claire (France)

May 1991
Vogue (Spain)

July 1992
Cosmopolitan (Germany)

August 1992
Harper's Bazaar

October 1992
Elle (Spain)

June 1993
Essence

January 1994
Elle (Spain)

December 1994
Elle

July 1995
Max

April 1996
TV-Spielfilm (Germany)

May 1996
Anna (Italy)

December 1996
GQ (Spain)

December 1996
Black Men

February 1997
Sports Illustrated

March 1997
Fitness

May 1997
Details

May 1997
Cosmopolitan (Germany)

July 1997
Cosmopolitan (Germany)

August 1997
Maxim

September 1997
Man (Spain)

November 1997
Photo (France)

December 1997
Shape

April 1998
Seventeen

July 1998
Photo (France)

July 1998
Cosmopolitan (Spain)

January 1999
GQ

April 1999
P.O.V.

July 1999
Black Men

February 2000
People

July 2000
Celebrity Sleuth

July 2000
Black Men

August 2000
Maxim

August 2000
Black Men

September 2000
TV Horen and Sehen (Germany)

October 2000
Total Film (Hungary)

June 2001
Miss Ebene (France)

May 2002
Ocean Drive

June 2002
Arena (United Kingdom)

July 2002
TV Direct (Germany)

September 2002
Ebony

November 2002
TV Guide

May 2003
Stuff

December 2003
People

March 2004
TV Guide

April 2004
King

May 2004
Ebony

January 2005
Vibe

September 2005
Self

April 2006
Redbook

June 2006
Lucky

May 2007
Time

July 2007
Tros Kompas (Netherlands)

September 2007
Ebony

February 2008
Entertainment Weekly

March 2008
New York Times Magazine

September 2008
Harper's Bazaar

December 2008
Ebony

February 2009
Elle Girl

Magazine Pictorials

February 1988
Elle

September 1990
Marie Claire (France)

March 1992
Glamour (Italy)

March 1992
Mademoiselle

July 1992
Mademoiselle

July 1992
Elle

September 1992
Vogue (United Kingdom)

October 1992
Vogue (United Kingdom)

October 1992
Elle

November 1992
Harper's Bazaar

November 1992
Elle

January 1993
Playboy

February 1993
Sports Illustrated

March 1993
Elle

June 1993
Seventeen

May 1994
Elle (United Kingdom)

February 1996
GQ

May 1996
Playboy

July 1996
Playboy

November 1996
Max

December 1996
Black Men

February 1997
Sports Illustrated

March 1997
Photo (France)

May 1997
Max

September 1997
Man

October 1997
GQ (United Kingdom)

February 1998
Sports Illustrated

Winter 1998
Sports Illustrated

June 1998
Photo (France)

January 1999
Max (Australia)

February 1999
Sports Illustrated

May 1999
Playboy

June 1999
Photo (France)

July 1999
GQ

January 2000
GQ

January 2000
Cinema (Hungary)

July 2000
Black Men

November 2000
Maxim

November 2000
Vox (Hungary)

December 2000
Playboy

November 2001
Celebrity Skin

March 2002
Celebrity Skin

November 2002
Sports Illustrated Ultimate Swimsuit Issue

February 2004
Sports Illustrated

March 2004
Playboy

July 2005
Playboy

March 2008
Playboy

September 2008
Harper's Bazaar

Appendix B

AWARDS

1994
Named one of *People* magazine's "50 Most Beautiful People in the World."

1996
Named one of *People* magazine's "100 Most Beautiful People in the World."

1997
Wins Michael Award as Supermodel of the Year.

1997
Awarded Starlight Foundation's "Friendship Award."

1999
Named "1999 Sally Beauty Supply's Best Tressed Celebrity" runner-up.

2000
Named GQ magazine's "Woman of the Year."

2000

Ranked #15 in *Playboy*'s "Sex Stars 2000."

2000

Named one of *Maxim* magazine's "Five For the Ages."

2000

Ranked #5 in *FHM*'s "100 Sexiest Women in the World 2000."

2001

Ranked #33 in *FHM*'s "100 Sexiest Women in the World 2001."

2004

Nominated for Teen Choice Award Choice Reality/Variety TV Star/ Female, for *America's Next Top Model*.

2005

Nominated for Teen Choice Award Choice TV Personality: Female.

2005

Named to *Fortune* magazine's "Celebrity 100 Power Ranking."

2006

Named one of *Time* magazine's "100 Most Influential People of the Year.

2007

Wins Teen Choice Award for *America's Next Top Model* and *The Tyra Banks Show*.

2006

Named to *Forbes* magazine's "Celebrity 100 Power Ranking."

2007

Nominated for Daytime Emmy Outstanding Talk Show/Informative.

2007

Named one of *Time* magazine's "100 Most Influential People of the Year."

2007
Awarded 2007 BET Award.

2008
Wins Daytime Emmy Outstanding Talk Show/Informative.

2008
Wins Teen Choice Award for *America's Next Top Model.*

2008
Named Top-Earning Female Entertainer by *Fortune* magazine.

2008
Nominated Daytime Emmy Outstanding Talk Show/Informative for *The Tyra Banks Show.*

2008
Named one of *Cosmopolitan* magazine's "2008 Fun Fearless Phenom" award winners.

2008
Named one of *Hollywood Reporter*'s "100 Most Powerful Women in Entertainment."

2008
Named one of *Entertainment Weekly*'s "25 Smartest in Television."

2008
Wins *Glamour* magazine's "Women of the Year Award."

2008
Named "Hardest-Working Celebrity in Show Business" by *Parade* magazine.

2009
Wins GLAAD Media Awards 2009 Excellence in Media award.

SELECTED BIBLIOGRAPHY

BOOKS, DOCUMENTARIES, MOVIES, AND TV SHOWS BY TYRA BANKS

America's Next Top Model. Co-produced by Ken Mok, Anthony Dominici, and Daniel Soiseth. Bankable Productions and Telepictures Productions, a division of Warner Bros. 2003–2009.

E! True Hollywood Story: Tyra Banks. Produced by Jeffrey Shore. E! Entertainment Television. 2005.

Honey Thunder Dunk. Produced by ABC's "Wonderful World of Disney." 1998. Disney Productions.

Stylista. Co-produced by Ken Mok. Bankable Productions and Warner Bros. 2008.

The Clique. Direct-to-DVD. Executive produced by Tyra Banks. A production of Warner Premiere. November 2008

The Tyra Banks Show. Co-produced by Ken Mok. Bankable Productions and Telepictures Productions, a division of Warner Bros. 2005–2009.

True Beauty. Co-produced by Denise Cramsey, Laura Armstrong, Ashton Kutcher, Jason Goldberg, Karey Burke, and Rod Aissa. Bankable Productions, Katalyst Productions, and Warner Horizon Television. 2009.

Tyra's Beauty Inside & Out. New York: Harper Collins, 1998.

"What Matters Most In My Work and My Life." *Newsweek*. October 13, 2008. www.newsweek.com.

BOOKS ABOUT TYRA BANKS

Chase, Lisa. *Totally Tyra: An Unauthorized Biography*. New York: Penguin Group, 2006.

Hill, Anne E. *Tyra Banks: From Supermodel to Role Model*. New York: Gateway Books, 2009.

Levin, Pam. *Tyra Banks*. Philadelphia: Chelsea House Publishers, 2000.

Schweitzer, Karen. *Tyra Banks, Modern Role Model*. Broomall, PA: Mason Crest Books, 2008.

ARTICLES ABOUT TYRA BANKS

Bennett, Joy. "The 15 Most Beautiful Black Women." *Ebony*. October 1, 1996. www.highbeam.com/doc/1G1-18736500.html.

Blakely, Kiri. "Tyra Banks on It." *Forbes*. July 2006. www.forbes.com/forbes/2006/0703/120.html.

Brown, Laura. "American Dream." *Harper's Bazaar*. September 2008. www.harpersbazaar.com/magazine/cover/tyra-banks-interview-0908.

Connor, Claire. "Why I Love My Body . . . Just the Way It Is." *Shape*. June 1, 2007. www.shape.com.

Gliatto, Tom. "Tyrasaurus." *People*, April 11, 1994. www.people.com/people/archive/article/0,,20107829,00.html.

Hirschberg, Lynn. "Banksable." *New York Times Magazine*, June 1, 2008. www.nytimes.com/2008/06/01/magazine/01tyra-t.html.

Klum, Heidi. *Time*, April 30, 2006. www.time.com/time/magazine/article/0,9171,1187401,00.html.

Martel, Ned. "For the Most Part, Far from the Modeling Crowd." *New York Times*, November, 2, 2005. www.nytimes.com/2005/11/02/arts/television/02mart.html.

Norment, Lynn. "Tyra Banks: On Top of the World." *Ebony*, May 1, 1997. www.highbeam.com/doc/1G1-19383832.html.

Ogunnaike, Lola. "My, What Pretty Claws." *New York Times*, September 26, 2004. www.nytimes.com/2004/09/26/fashion/26TYRA .html

Roberts, Michael. "America's Next Top Mogul." *Vanity Fair*. February 2007. www.vanityfair.com/fame/features/video/2007/tyra _video200701.

Samuels, Adrienne P. "Tyra Unexpected: Smart but Not Cheap, Tyra Banks Swears She's Just and Ordinary Lady." *Ebony*, December 1, 2008. www.highbeam.com/doc/1G1-189551743.html.

Serwer, Andy. "From Top Model to Young Oprah." *Fortune*, February 15, 2006. http://money.cnn.com/magazines/fortune/fortune _archive/2006/02/20/8369125/index.htm.

Stack, Tim. "America's Next Top Mogul." *Entertainment Weekly*, February 22, 2008. www.ew.com/ew/article/0,,20178169,00.html.

"Tyra Banks Building an Empire." *The Cincinnati Post*, December 5, 2005. www.highbeam.com/doc/1G1-140063194.html.

Wheaton, Sarah, "The Hillary-Tyra Show." *New York Magazine*, January 16, 2008. http://thecaucus.blogs.nytimes.com/2008/01/16/the-hillary-tyra-show/.

BOOKS ON ADVERTISING, BLACK HISTORY, AND MODELING

Frum, David. *How We Got Here: The '70s*. New York: Basic Books, 2000.

Schulberg, Jay. *The Milk Mustache Book*. New York: Ballantine Books, 1998.

Summers, Barbara. *Skin Deep: Inside the World of Black Fashion Models*. New York: Amisted Press, 1999.

Thomas, Duane. *Soul Style: Black Women Redefining the Color of Fashion*. Hagerstown, MD: University Publishing, 2000.

INTERNET

Albiniak, Paige. "Bank on Tyra: Fashion Shows Are a Safe Bet." *The Early Show*. November 29, 2004. www.theearlyshow.com.

America's Next Top Model. www.cwtv.com/shows/americas-next-top-model

"Bristol Palin's Ex Says They Don't Get Along." *AP Worldstream*. April 6, 2008. www.highbeam.com/doc/1A1-D97B6K2O0.html.

Eng, Joyce. "Vanessa Minnillo Finds the Beauty Within." *TV Guide.com*. January 1, 2009. www.tvguide.com/News/Vanessa-Minnillo-Previews-1001218.aspx.

Gispon, Ni'Cole.. "UPN Picks Up a Second Cycle of America's Next Top Model." *PRNewswire*. June 25, 2003. http://www2 .prnewswire.com/cgi-bin/stories.pl?ACCT=104&STORY=/ www/story/06-25-2003/0001971931&EDATE=.

Recano, Victoria. "The Insider Goes One-on-One with Tyra Banks." September 16, 2008. www.theinsider.com/videos/1194873 _The_Insider_Goes_One_on_One_with_Tyra_Banks.

Richmond, Ray. "True Beauty TV Review." *The Hollywood Reporter*. January 6, 2009. www.hollywoodreporter.com/hr/tv-reviews/ true-beauty-tv-review-1003927235.story.

News.com. September 16, 2008. www.theinsidernews.com.

Tyra.com. www.tyra.com.

The Tyra Banks Show Web site. www.tyrashow.com.

INDEX

Acceptance to college, 16–17. *See
also* Loyola Marymount
University
Advocate, The: Alexander, Jay
Manual, 86; National Coming
Out Day, 86; transgender episode,
86–87. *See also* Alexander, Jay
Manual; Gay marriage
African Americans in
entertainment during the 1970s, 2
Alcohol and drinking, Tyra's views
on, 9, 49
Alexander, Jay Manual: gay makeup
artist, judge and runway coach for
America's Next Top Model, 65;
reaction to Tyra's job offer,
111–12
America's Next Top Model: first show
preparation, 112; inspiration for,
63; marketing, 63–64; media
critiques, 146; Mok, Ken,
co-producer, 64; premiere of, 65;
ratings, 64–65; sale to UPN, 64;
syndication of, 66; Tyra's role in,
65–66. *See also* Mok, Ken
"America's Next Top Waddle": in

Australian tabloid, 81–82; So
What campaign, 83–84; Tyra's
media rebuttals, 82–85. *See also*
Kiss My Fat Ass
Ames, Jackie, 31–32. *See also* First
movie role; *Fresh Prince of Bel-Air,
The*; Smith, Will.
Aunt Sharon, 6–7. *See also*
Childhood health problems

Bankable, Inc., founding of, 27;
renamed from Ty Girl
Corporation, 27
Bankable Productions, 64. *See also*
Paratore, James; UPN
Banks, Carolyn (mother), 1;
co-founder of Tyra Banks Foundation, 27; co-founder of TZone,
136; divorce from Banks, Don, 4–
5; frugality lessons, 10; encourages
young Tyra in her modeling
career, 14–15; joins Tyra in Paris
to guide her career, 25; photographs Tyra's modeling portfolio,
22; works with Tyra on perfecting
runway strut, 22

Banks, Devin (brother): Tyra's adult
    relationship with, 27; Air Force
    medic, 27; Tyra's childhood
    relationship with, 1; 3–4, 9–10
Banks, Don (biological father):
    Tyra's adult relationship with, 27;
    computer consultant, 1; divorce
    from mother Carolyn, 4–5
Banxxx, Tyra: guest/porn star Tyra
    Banks impersonator on *The Tyra
    Banks Show*, 74; *Xtreme* magazine,
    75
Basketball, Tyra's love of: as fan of
    Los Angeles Lakers, 57; portraying
    basketball star in *Honey Thunder
    Dunk*, . 57–58. *See also* Women's
    National Basketball Association
"BBQ" (Tyra's TZone nickname),
    55, 137
Bowers, Marci. M.D.: guest surgeon
    on *America's Next Top Model*, 88;
    offers to pay for transgender
    surgery of King, Isis, 88. *See also*
    King, Isis.
Boys n the Hood, 36. *See also*
    Singleton, John
Breakout modeling role, Tyra's, 21.
    See also Seventeen Magazine
Business savvy, Tyra's: as an actress,
    36; as "America's Next Top
    Mogul," 102, 146; as co-founder
    of Tyra Banks Foundation, 27;
    as co-founder of TZone, 56; as
    co-producer/host of *America's
    Next Top Model*, 63; as co-
    producer/host of *The Tyra Banks
    Show*, 74, 86, 131; on *Forbes*'s list
    of top earners, 102, 146–47. *See
    also* Bankable, Inc.; Bankable
    Productions; *Ebony* magazine;

Forbes magazine; Ty Girl
    Corporation

Campbell, Naomi: guest on
    America's Next Top Model for
    public reconciliation with Tyra,
    145; supermodel rivalry with Tyra,
    17, 30; Victoria's Secret
    supermodel, 81, 108–9
Carey, Mariah, 107
Chanel, modeling for: banned from
    runway by Campbell, Naomi, 17,
    110; in Paris, 23, 25
Changing image of African
    American women in the media,
    51–52
Charities, Tyra's: Center for
    Children & Families, 44;
    Children's Hope Foundation, 51;
    Friendship Award, 136; Kidshare
    Toy Drive; 44; Starlight
    Children's Foundation, 44;
    surrogate children, 44; *See also*
    Tyra Banks Foundation; Tyra
    Banks Scholarship Fund; TZone
Childhood health problems:
    benchwarmer, 13; towers over
    friends and teachers, 13; under-
    weight, 10–11; warts, 6. *See also*
    Growth spurt, adolescent;
    Lightbulb Head; Olive Oyl.
Cigarettes/smoking, Tyra's criticism
    of: dangers of peer pressure, 9;
    smoking to stay thin, 9; turns
    down lucrative tobacco ads, 8;
    witnesses grandmother Florine
    London's death from lung
    cancer, 8
Clinton, Hillary: guest/presidential
    candidate on *The Tyra Banks*

Show, 125–26; talks about husband Bill Clinton's affair with Monica Lewinsky, 126

Clique, The, producer of, 94

Cocaine, 74. *See also* Illegal Drugs, Tyra's stance on; Moss, Kate

Cosmopolitan magazine: "Fun Fearless Phenoms award," 89–90; Tyra cover story, 81–82

CoverGirl, contract with, 30

Crawford, Cindy: MTV host-role model, 22; Pepsi ad with Tyra; 39; supermodel role model, 29–30, 114

Current boyfriend (Tyra's), Utendahl, John, 117

CW network: launched by *The Tyra Banks Show*, 64; *Stylista* debut, 95

"Daddy's Little Girl," 3–5, 54

Dating disasters: Derek, 13–14; no more model groupies, 56; Seal, 116

Daytime Emmy Awards, 81; *The Tyra Banks Show*, first to win in its category, 93

Deja, 36. *See also Higher Learning*; Singleton, John

Dickinson, Janice: criticism of Tyra, 66, 89, 91; fired by Tyra from *America's Next Top Model*, 144–45. *See also* Judges, *America's Next Top Model*

Disadvantaged teenage girls, Tyra's work with: Tyra Banks Foundation, 54, 136; Tyra Banks Scholarship Fund, 27, 136; TZone, 54–56, 60, 136; Volunteerism awards, 50–51. *See also* Charities, Tyra's

Divorce, parents, 5. *See also* Banks, Carolyn; Banks, Don

Drugs, illegal, Tyra's stance on, 9, 25, 35, 52, 55, 74, 109. *See also* Moss, Kate

Early Show, The, Tyra coverage, 65–67; 70–71; 76

Eating disorders in the modeling industry, 108, 114–15

Ebony magazine: "15 Most Beautiful Black Women," 135; Tyra coverage, 39, 50, 59, 102–3, 140–42, 146–48

Edwards, John, guest/presidential candidate on *The Tyra Banks Show*, 127–29, 134

Elite Model Management, 16, 21, 68

Emerging role of Black women in the 1970s, 2

Empire, Tyra wants to build, 46, 59, 147

Employees, Tyra's relationship with, 103

Entertainment Weekly, "America's Next Top Mogul," 102, 111–12, 120, 146

Family values, 4–5. *See also* Banks, Carolyn; Banks, Devin; Banks, Don; Charities; Johnson, Clifford, Jr.

Fashion industry, Tyra's experience with: breaking through racial barriers, 110; disservice to women, 146; eating disorders rampant in, 115–16; public criticism of, on talk show, 12, 39, 44. *See also* Kiss My Fat Ass; So What campaign; Weight struggles

"Fat Suit" episode, 73–74. *See also Tyra Banks Show, The*; Weight struggles

Final modeling gig, 81. *See also* Victoria's Secret

Financial Success, Tyra's: charities, 136; commercial success, 39; *Forbes*'s "Celebrity 100 List," 79; Oprah's role in, 75; views about money, 103, 141. *See also* Banks, Carolyn; Charities; Supermodel career; Thriftiness, Tyra's; Tyra Banks Scholarship Fund; TZone

First movie role, 86–88, 127. *See also* Ames, Jackie; *Fresh Prince of Bel-Air, The*; Smith, Will

First magazine cover, 23. *See also 20 Ans*

First modeling agency, 21. *See also* L.A. Models

Food/dieting: Tyra's childhood food favorites, 4; Tyra's healthy adult food favorites, 139; Tyra's fast food cravings as a supermodel in Paris, 24. *See also* Eating disorders; Retires from modeling; Weight struggles

Forbes magazine: "Celebrity 100 List," 79–80; "Top Female Performer," 146, 149; Tyra coverage, 102, 107–8

Fresh Prince of Bel-Air, The, 31–32, 57. *See also* Ames, Jackie; Smith, Will

"Froggy" (childhood nickname), 6. *See also* Childhood health problems

Gay marriage, Tyra's views on, 127. *See also* Huckabee, Mike

Glamour magazine: "2008 Women of the Year," 56; Tyra coverage, 56, 102

Green, Brady, 118. *See also* Stalker

Growth spurt, adolescent, 113. *See also* Lightbulb Head; Olive Oyl

GQ magazine: "GQ Woman of the Year," 38–40; Tyra coverage, 30, 116, 135

Hackner, Lisa, 70–71. *See also America's Next Top Model*; UPN

Hair: effects of modeling on hair health, 113; Tyra's bad hair days, 112–13; Tyra's childhood hair disasters, 12; Tyra's "off-duty" hairstyles, 27

Harper's Bazaar magazine: Tyra channels Michelle Obama, 128–29; Tyra compared to Martha Stewart, 138; Tyra coverage, 27–28, 133, 140, 147

Healthy lifestyle habits, 52, 139

Higher Learning, 13, 35, 37, 117. *See also* Deja; Singleton, John

Hollywood Reporter, "100 Most Powerful Women in Hollywood," 102

Homes, Tyra's, 39, 49, 118

Honey Thunder Dunk, 57–58. *See also* Wonderful World of Disney

Huckabee, Mike, 126–27, 129. *See also* Politics

Humility, Tyra's views on, 55, 99

Immaculate Heart High School, 11; high school uniform, 14; no boys, 11; scholarship, 44; Tyra's friendship with Khefri Riley, 14–15; Tyra's prom dress, 15; Tyra's rejection from modeling agencies in senior year, 15; Tyra's transfer to, 11. *See also* Tyra Banks Scholarship Fund

Inglewood, California: birthplace, 1; fond memories of, 4; home of Los Angeles Lakers, 1

International Children's School, 5

Interviewing style, Tyra's, 143

John Burroughs Middle School, 11

Johnson, Clifford, Jr. (stepfather), 10; Tyra's adult relationship with, 12; Tyra's childhood discipline problems with, 10–11

Johnston, Levi, guest on *The Tyra Banks Show*, 130–31. *See also* Palin, Bristol

Judges, *America's Next Top Model*: Alexander, Jay Manual; 65–67; Dickinson, Janice, 65; Porizkova, Paula, 65; Quillian, Beau, 65; Simmons, Kimora Lee, 66, 111

King, Isis: guest on *America's Next Top Model*, 87–88; Walls, Darrell, 87. *See also* Bowers, Marci, M.D.; Transgenders

Kiss My Fat Ass, 81–84; Secret Service acronym, 129; So What campaign, 83. *See also* Food; Retires from modeling; Weight struggles

Klum, Heidi: friend and supermodel mentor, 68; host of *Project Runway*, 68, 102; Victoria's Secret angel, 40. *See also* Project Runway

L.A. Models, 16, 21. *See also* First modeling agency; *Seventeen* magazine

Lightbulb Head, 11, 112–13. *See also* Growth spurt, adolescent; Olive Oyl

London, Florine (grandmother), 8. *See also* Cigarettes/smoking

Loyola Marymount University, 21. *See also* Tyra Banks Scholarship Fund

Marcaccini, Giancarlo (boyfriend), 117

Mentors, 29–30, 55, 69–70, 71, 73, 95, 102, 114, 136; Brady, James, 69–70; Leno, Jay, 69–70; Simmons, Kimora Lee, 66, 111. *See also* Klum, Heidi; Schiffer, Claudia; Stewart, Martha; Tiegs, Cheryl; Winfrey, Oprah

Miami Times, Tyra coverage, 72, 77, 138, 148

Milk mustache ads, 42–43, 46, 109, 119

Minnillo, Vanessa, 99–100. *See also* True Beauty

Modeling agencies, Tyra's: Elite Model Management, 21–22; L.A. Models, 15–17; unrealistic expectations about weight and appearance, 108–10.

Mok, Ken: co-producer , 63–64; views on gays, 87; views on Tyra, 141–42. *See also* America's Next Top Model; Tyra Banks Show, The

Moss, Kate: cocaine bust, 74; milk mustache ad, 42

"Most Beautiful Black Women Award," 135, 147

"Most Beautiful People Award," 33,
101, 135
Music, Tyra's favorite, 57
Music video roles, 55

New York Post, Tyra coverage, 64,
79, 85–86, 90. 141–45
New York Times Magazine, Tyra
coverage, 98–99, 102–3

Obama, Barack, guest on *The Tyra
Banks Show*, 123–25. *See also*
Politics
Obama, Michelle, as portrayed by
Tyra in *Harper's Bazaar*, 128
Olive Oyl, 11–12, 112. *See also*
Growth spurt, adolescent

Palin, Bristol, 130–34
Palin, Sarah, 129–30
Paratore, James, 64, 67. *See also*
UPN; Warner Brothers
Paris modeling career: breakthrough
offer, 22; feud with Campbell,
Naomi, 25; homesickness, 24;
mother joins Tyra, 25–26;
"outcast," 23–25; overnight
success, 23; *20 Ans*, 23. *See also*
Banks, Carolyn; Campbell,
Naomi; Chanel; Eating disorders;
First magazine cover; Food;
Supermodel career
People magazine, Tyra coverage, 15,
22, 27, 82–83
Pepsi contract, 29–30, 39
Politics, presidential interviews,
123–29, 131, 133
Porizkova, Paulina, 66. *See also*
Judges, *America's Next Top Model*
Producer, Tyra: *Clique, The*, 93;

Honey Thunder Dunk, 57; *Stylista*,
94–98; *True Beauty*, 99–101;
Warner Brothers production
deal, 93
Project Runway, 68, 102. *See also*
Klum, Heidi

Racism, Tyra's experience with, 24,
109; in early modeling career,
22–23
Reality TV: awards, 81; big break,
111; fan of, 63; franchise with, 67;
idea for *America's Next Top Model*,
65; launch of CW network, 93;
mentors, 71, 73; role of Oprah,
75–77; salary, 79; UPN, 111. *See
also America's Next Top Model*;
Stylista; *True Beauty*; *Tyra Banks
Show, The*
Retires from modeling, 79
Riley, Khefri, 15
Roadblocks encountered in
modeling, 108–11
Role models: 29–30, 55, 69–70, 71,
73, 95, 102, 114, 136. *See also*
Klum, Heidi; Schiffer, Claudia;
Stewart, Martha; Tiegs, Cheryl;
Winfrey, Oprah

Sawyer, Diane, interviews with, 28,
65, 82
Schiffer, Claudia, as role model, 29–
30, 114
Self-esteem, Tyra's interest in pro-
moting: importance of maintaining during weight gain and tabloid
exposure, 85; as a supermodel, 53–
54; working with young girls, 36;
working with young women, 138.
See also Food; Kiss My Fat Ass; So

What campaign; Tyra Banks
Foundation; Tyra Banks Scholar-
ship Fund; TZone; Weight
struggles
Sense of humor, Tyra's: during
presidential interviews, 132;
importance in maintaining, 38;
important trait in men, 57–58
Seventeen magazine, 4. *See also* L.A.
Models
Sex, Tyra's views on, 51–52, 130,
145; "Sexiest Women," 135
Singing career, Tyra's, 58, 107–8
Singleton, John, 32, 35–36, 45, 117
Slowey, Anne: media criticism, 104;
in *Stylista*, 95–97, 99
Smith, Will, 31. *See also* Ames,
Jackie; First movie role; *Fresh
Prince of Bel-Air, The*
So What campaign, 83. *See also*
Food; Kiss My Fat Ass; Weight
struggles
Sports Illustrated Swimsuit Issue: first
African American cover model,
38–40; post-runway weight gain,
135, 139; *Sports Illustrated 1998
Swimsuit Calendar*, 40
Stalker, 14, 17, 21, 54, 58, 136. *See
also* Green, Brady
Stepfather, 10, 27. *See also* Johnson,
Clifford, Jr.
Stewart, Martha: as role model, 75,
102; Tyra compared to, 138; Tyra
wants an empire like her, 146–47
Stylista: *Elle* magazine, 95;
inspiration for, 95; media
critiques, 97–99; premiere, 95;
Slowey, Anne, 95–100
Supermodel career: CoverGirl, 29–
30, 33; during year in Paris, 22–26;

early rejections suffered, 21;
magazine covers done, 27;
Victoria's Secret, 28. *See also*
Cosmopolitan magazine; *Ebony*
magazine; *Forbes* magazine; *GQ*
magazine; Kiss My Fat Ass; Paris
modeling career; *People* magazine;
So What campaign; *Sports
Illustrated* Swimsuit Issue;
Victoria's Secret; Weight struggles
Swatch contract, 43, 46

Telepictures, career with, 69–71
Television commercials, 30, 39; L'il
Penny, 39; milk mustache ads,
42–43
Three Million Dollar Bra, 41, 46. *See
also* Victoria's Secret
Thriftiness, Tyra's, 140–41. *See also*
Banks, Carolyn; Business savvy;
Empire, Tyra's
Tiegs, Cheryl, as role model, 30
Tobacco ads, Tyra's refusal to do, 9.
See also Cigarettes/smoking
Transgender contestants, 86, 88. *See
also* King, Isis
True Beauty: inspiration for, 99;
media criticism, 100–101;
Minnillo, Vanessa, host of,
99–101
TV Guide, Tyra coverage, 99–100,
104, 133
20 Ans, 23. *See also* First magazine
cover; Paris modeling career
Ty Girl Corporation, 10, 27. *See also*
Bankable, Inc.
Tyra Banks Foundation, 54. *See also*
TZone
Tyra Banks Scholarship Fund, 27,
136

Tyra Banks Show, The: Clinton, Hillary, 125–26; Daytime Emmy award, 81, 93; endermologie, 73; "Fat Suit" episode, 73–74; Huckabee, Mike, 126–27; Johnston, Levi, 130–31; King, Isis, 87–88; media critiques, 71–72; Moss, Kate, 73; Obama, Barack, 123–25; Palin, Bristol, 130–34; premiere, 71; sonogram, 73; Tyra Banxxx, 74

Tyra Porkchops, 82, 139. *See also* Food; Kiss My Fat Ass; So What Campaign; Weight struggles

Tyra's Beauty Inside & Out: bad hair and beauty days, 112; book debut, 51; importance of helping others, 44; "self-help book for teens," 5; teenage dating woes, 13; volunteer work, 136

TZone: camp counselor, 60; first summer, 60–61; founding of, 54–56, 136. *See also* Self-esteem; Tyra Banks Foundation; Weight struggles

UPN, 67, 70, 93, 111, 144. *See also* CW network

Utendahl, John, 117. *See also* Current boyfriend

Vanity Fair, Tyra coverage, 69, 76

Victoria's Secret: cyber fashion show, 40–42; first African-American woman to grace catalogue cover, 38; Tyra retiring from, 79–81; Tyra's contract with, 29. *See also* Three Million Dollar Bra

Washington Post, Tyra coverage, 63, 91, 98, 104, 132, 134, 137

Warner Brothers, 64, 70, 94

Weight struggles: photo shoot challenges with, 39; post-runway weight gain, 139; tabloid exposure of, 82–84. *See also* Kiss My Fat Ass; Retires from modeling; So What campaign

Winfrey, Oprah: honors shared with Tyra, 135; inspiration and training for Tyra's own talk show, 63, 75; mentor, 69; "The Next Oprah," 79, 101–2, 143; Tyra as youth correspondent for, 58–59

Women's National Basketball Association: as portrayed in *Honey Thunder Dunk*, 57; Tyra as spokesperson for, 57

Wonderful World of Disney, 57. *See also Honey Thunder Dunk*

Workout regime, Tyra's: following her doctor's orders, 140; with dance and drums, 57; with mother, Carolyn, 7. *See also* Food; Weight struggles

Youth correspondent for Oprah's show, 58

About the Author

CAROLE JACOBS is an award-winning writer and author who specializes in travel, health, fitness, and celebrities. A former 20-year senior editor and founding travel editor for *Shape* magazine and 3-year travel editor for *Shape*'s sister publication, *Living Fit*, Carole's freelance articles have appeared in 250-plus magazines and in major newspapers across North America through United Press Syndicate. She has authored several books on a variety of health and nutrition topics, including the just-published *Detox for the Rest of Us*, *The Everything Guide to Juicing*, and *The Everything Guide to Adult ADHD*, and also coauthored a travel guide for Reader's Digest Books and a women's fitness guide for G. P. Putnam. Carole is currently the fitness travel editor for *Travelgirl* magazine.